LIPS

Constance Congdon

BROADWAY PLAY PUBLISHING INC
New York
www.broadwayplaypublishing.com
info@broadwayplaypublishing.com

LIPS
© Copyright 2000 by Constance Congdon

All rights reserved. This work is fully protected under the copyright laws of the United States of America. No part of this publication may be photocopied, reproduced, stored in a retrieval system, or transmitted, in any form or by any means, electronic, mechanical, recording, or otherwise, without the prior permission of the publisher. Additional copies of this play are available from the publisher.

Written permission is required for live performance of any sort. This includes readings, cuttings, scenes, and excerpts. For amateur and stock performances, please contact Broadway Play Publishing Inc. For all other rights please contact the author c/o B P P I.

Book design: Marie Donovan
Page make-up: Adobe InDesign
Typeface: Palatino

LIPS was written under the Dreamworks/Playwrights Horizons play commissioning program and received readings at The Missoula Colony at Montana Rep, at Playwrights Horizons, and a fully-produced workshop, directed by Peter Lobdell, at Amherst College.

LIPS was first produced by Primary Stages (Casey Childs, Artistic Director) in New York City on 14 April 1999. The cast and creative contributors were:

RACHEL.. Robin Morse
ANDY .... Stephen Barker Turner
JONI .... Lizbeth Mackay
*SECRET SERVICE AGENTS........ Phil Horton & John Power

Director .... Greg Leaming
Set design .... Rob Ordorisio
Costume design .... Mary Myers
Lighting design .... Jeff Croiter
Original music/sound .... Fabian Obispo

non-speaking roles added to facilitate scene changes

Acknowlegements: Peter Lobdell, Molly Hemsley, Brian Quinn, Linda McInerney and the Department of Theater and Dance at Amherst College. Also Susan Cole and Elizabeth Mulcahy.

ACT ONE

Scene One

(RACHEL *is in a sterile-looking office-like room, sitting and smoking, facing front. She's wearing rumpled casual garb. Beside her is a plastic garbage bag filled with her belongings.* ANDY *enters the room from behind. He's in a suit and tie. She knows he's there, but doesn't turn around. She's not angry, but oozes bored, bad attitude.*)

ANDY: There's no smoking here.

RACHEL: There's no smoking everywhere.

ANDY: Are you going to put it out?

RACHEL: Where are the ashtrays?

ANDY: We don't have any.

RACHEL: Why not?

ANDY: Because there's no smoking here.

RACHEL: So…if someone is smoking, where are they supposed to put their cigarette out?

ANDY: No one smokes here.

(RACHEL *points to her lit cigarette.*)

RACHEL: Hellooooooo.

ANDY: *(Just the greeting)* Hello.

(RACHEL *just looks at* ANDY.)

ANDY: Long time…

(RACHEL *turns away.*)

RACHEL: Curb the clichés. This room—your suit—are enough.

ANDY: Nice luggage. Vuitton?

(RACHEL *chooses not to acknowledge* ANDY's *"score."*)

RACHEL: Even the best computer programs have a command series to accommodate the— (*She takes a big puff of her cigarette and blows it out, with great pleasure.*) —anomaly. And why? For the OVERALL efficiency of the ENTIRE program.

ANDY: (*Finds something in the trash*) Here. Put it out in here.

RACHEL: That's not an ashtray. That's a juice box.

ANDY: Just put the cigarette in the hole—there's enough liquid left to put it out.

RACHEL: It'll smell.

ANDY: It'll work.

RACHEL: And now the anomaly is reduced—and I do mean reduced—to doing things that, to her, are degrading. To ask me to put my cigarette in the hole where a little child is supposed to put a straw? And what is not lost on me is the infantilisation of what could be a vagina recast as an opening in a small box—a container that has meant many things to many people for ages, but never as a place to keep— (*Reads label on juice box*) —"cranberry juice." Well, at least there are some women on the premises. And then the further degrading experience of putting my cigarette into something that came from the garbage and will return to same, smelling really bad, reduces me to the status of some hooker in the bus station.

ANDY: You mean "sex worker."

(*Pause*)

ACT ONE

RACHEL: So you've had that sensitivity training they give to government employees. Good.

ANDY: My mother's a feminist.

RACHEL: Isn't that like saying, "Some of my best friends are Black?"

ANDY: My mother teaches feminist theory. She just got tenure.

RACHEL: And she's still a feminist—wo.

ANDY: I'm proud of her.

RACHEL: Is she proud of you?

ANDY: Sure.

RACHEL: What's the world coming to?

ANDY: Sanity.

RACHEL: You're the only person in the world who believes that.

ANDY: *(About the cigarette)* You're going to burn your fingers. *(He takes the cigarette and tries to stuff it through the hole in the juice box)*

RACHEL: You're making a mess.

ANDY: That's why we need you.

RACHEL: Oh, don't even try. *(Pause)* Oh, that was so lame!

ANDY: So are you going to cooperate?

RACHEL: No.

ANDY: I think you have to.

RACHEL: I can't.

ANDY: Why not?

RACHEL: Because I can't be near this issue. I can't have some people thinking I'm...that way.

ANDY: Why not? You're an ex-con— *(Looks at watch)* —by about five and a half hours ago. Is "this issue" worse?

RACHEL: To some people—yes, absolutely.

ANDY: What if "those people" knew you were working for us?

RACHEL: What? In a new Cabinet position? Secretary of the Interior? Yo.

ANDY: You'd be a sexual spy. Your sexuality— whatever it is—

RACHEL: "Whatever it is?" You forgot?

ANDY: —wouldn't be the issue. The point is you'd be working for us—

RACHEL: "Us." Oh, it's "us." Of course. Well—what is your name again? Andy?—right. Well, "they" wouldn't believe it—that I was working for you. Because anyone who knows me well, knows that I hate the fucking government. And I hate this administration. One of her suits—ONE of her outfits— could feed a family of four for six months!

ANDY: I agree—she needs policing. Clothing budgets are just indicative of other…excesses. And that's what we want to know about. Excesses, relationships, that could be problems or ammunition, depending on their use. Knowledge is power and in this town, it's turbo power. We binged and purged and now we're due for another cycle. We are a bulimic nation.

RACHEL: Listen to the way you sound. You just said a whole bunch of crap and I have NO IDEA what you're talking about.

ANDY: We need to watch her. And you have to help.

RACHEL: I don't have to do anything. Except bodily functions. And die.

ACT ONE

ANDY: Taxes.

RACHEL: I'm exempt. For now.

ANDY: So if you don't do this, where will you live? Move in with your mother?

RACHEL: I have resources.

ANDY: Not many prisoners get a job offer on the day of their release.

RACHEL: There are programs I can go into. There's a structure—for women—like me.

ANDY: There is no one like you.

(Beat. RACHEL does hear the compliment, but doesn't trust it.)

RACHEL: Why, Andy—why are you doing this? What's your…payoff?

ANDY: My job—is to find out if you can be into this. Because it won't work, unless you're into it.

RACHEL: So you require my belief as well as my brain?

ANDY: And your heart and your soul.

RACHEL: So that confirms your identity. The only thing left to discuss is the price.

ANDY: We know the price. You paid it already.

RACHEL: So I just meet her?

ANDY: At first. And if you think you can do it, you go further and we find out what we need to know. Period. You're a spy. And paid. Well. And you have a choice in your life.

RACHEL: Choice is just another form of maya.

ANDY: What does this have to do with pyramids in the jungle?

RACHEL: I meant the Sanskrit word for "illusion."

(*Long beat. She emits an audible breath, looks at him. He leans towards her to make certain she really hears his next words.*)

ANDY: Think of the restaurants.

(*End of scene*)

Scene Two

(*Lights up on a good restaurant—wine and two places set with food that has been partially consumed.* ANDY *is finishing his dinner.* RACHEL *enters—she's been out smoking—and sits back down at her unfinished dinner. She's tipsy.*)

RACHEL: They made me go all the way outside.

ANDY: Give it up. It will simplify your life.

RACHEL: So is that your solution for the world? "Everyone, just get over everything. Eastern Europe—forget history. Actually, everyone, forget history. Take a deep cleansing breath—" (*She breathes out fully to demonstrate—it makes her cough.*) And isn't that the fucking problem. History is still in our lungs!

ANDY: I think you've had too much to drink.

RACHEL: You are the date from Hell.

(*Beat.* ANDY *doesn't respond.*)

RACHEL: You are so controlling. How do you work with people?

ANDY: I let you go outside by yourself.

RACHEL: You didn't want to leave your dinner.

(*Beat*)

ANDY: How's your salmon?

ACT ONE

RACHEL: I should have gotten the dill sauce, or whatever it was, on the side.

ANDY: Drink some wine to clear your palate. Not too much more, though.

RACHEL: Problem—Solution. Relentless Control.

ANDY: They're here.

RACHEL: Where?

ANDY: Table four.

RACHEL: "Table Four"? Which one?

ANDY: By the big ficus.

(Pause as she looks at him.)

RACHEL: What the fuck is a "ficus"?

ANDY: It's a fig tree with delicate leaves. It's in a teal-colored jardiniere—in the corner.

RACHEL: Are you gay?

ANDY: No.
I'm ordering you some coffee.

RACHEL: I'm fine. Okay. Whatever. *(She turns around slowly, so as not to "call attention to herself" and looks for Table Four. She sees it and turns back.)*

RACHEL: Jesus…

ANDY: *(Signalling to order from an offstage waiter)* Coffee?!

RACHEL: Jesus.

ANDY: Are you all right?

RACHEL: They look so nice.

ANDY: Yes?

RACHEL: But so did Bonnie and Clyde.

ANDY: You don't have to con yourself.
There are lots of good reasons to do things.

RACHEL: You're paternalistic. And prissy. Weird.

ANDY: Bonnie and Clyde were poor white trash—they just dressed well.

RACHEL: Are you kidding? Bonnie looked great. He's the one who looked like a hick.

ANDY: I'm not talking about the old movie.

RACHEL: Duh. Neither am I. I saw the photographs—have you ever seen the photographs? They were crazy about each other, having such a good time.

ANDY: They're hardly Bonnie and Clyde. They're not really criminals—in spite of what some might say. You, however, are, and in spite of—

RACHEL: In spite of what?

ANDY: Your obvious, superior intelligence.

RACHEL: Okay—that's so classist—or something. Anyway, it's wrong. And insulting to all people of ordinary intelligence who are or aren't criminals or something I can't quite track right now. And I'm not anything like Bonnie and Clyde. I don't like being in the same breath with them—I've never killed anyone. I just...manipulated some numbers.

ANDY: You won't even have to do that. *(Looking for the waiter again)* Coffee? Please? Over here?

(RACHEL *looks back at Table Four.*)

RACHEL: She looks so nice.

ANDY: It'll be pleasant, then.

RACHEL: Where's my coffee? Did you order my coffee?

ANDY: It's on its way.
Don't look at her again. She'll suspect something.

RACHEL: Doesn't she have someone guarding her?

ACT ONE

ANDY: There are men everywhere.

RACHEL: What about when she has to go the bathroom? Who protects her there?

ANDY: I guess they don't worry about that.

RACHEL: Well, they should. People underestimate us all the time. And they goddam shouldn't.

ANDY: I'm going to get that coffee. Stay here.

RACHEL: What am I? Your dog? Fuck you.

ANDY: We're going.

RACHEL: I want dessert.

ANDY: *(Waves toward the offstage waiter)* Check. *(Can't get the waiter's attention)*

RACHEL: What's a boy to do? Put an embargo on the restaurant! Cut off their foreign trade. No more escargot! No more Chateau Neuf Whatever.

ANDY: We've leaving. Come on…

(He stands and tries to get her up. She pulls away.)

RACHEL: Touch me again and see what happens.

ANDY: This is obviously not working out.

RACHEL: I'm going to the ladies room.
Bluto.
Sit.

(RACHEL waits. ANDY sits down slowly. She exits. He looks slightly toward Table Four, then goes to get the waiter.)

(End of scene)

Scene Three

(Lights up in a corner of the ladies room. Sound of retching, then flushing. RACHEL comes out of one of the stalls and goes to the trash receptacle behind the door—out of the way,

anyway—takes out some mouthwash, swallows it, spits it out in the trash, then looks around to see if she's alone and takes out a small mirror and some cocaine. She quickly spreads the coke on the mirror, makes a line and snorts it. Just then, JONI *enters. She's wiping her hands with some packaged finger wipes restaurants serve with messy food— she sees* RACHEL *and speaks to her)*

JONI: Lobster is so messy. I shouldn't eat it. Do you eat lobster?

RACHEL: No.

JONI: They're...bottom feeders, you know. So you eat whatever they ate. And in this world, that could be anything. Could I borrow your little mirror? I'm trying to see what's in my eye...

(RACHEL *is frozen there.* JONI *reaches over and picks up* RACHEL'S *small mirror. She runs her finger over the surface, picking up whatever coke is left and then she spreads it on her gums.)*

JONI: That's the only thing I miss. That tingly smile. *(She hands her back the mirror.)* So, the suit you're with: pushing thirty—fairly well hung—never married— okay in bed—loves oral intercourse. Always wears a condom—unless you're blowing him, of course. Watch yourself.

RACHEL: Okay.

JONI: *(About the cocaine)* And don't ski here—it's the South, darling—they hate snow. There's surveillance everywhere in our little...village.

RACHEL: Oh, I get it from my roommate and I don't live...there any more. With her.

(Long pause)

JONI: Is anyone trying to kill me?

RACHEL: No, ma'am.

ACT ONE   11

(JONI *moves to* RACHEL, *takes* RACHEL's *face in her hands, and kisses her passionately on the mouth.*)

JONI: Mmmm—mouth wash.
Keep me informed. Here's my private number.

(JONI *puts the card into* RACHEL's *bra and then exits. After a beat,* ANDY *enters the ladies room.*)

ANDY: Why did you have to come in here?

RACHEL: I was sick.

ANDY: You're so naive.

RACHEL: I quit.

(RACHEL *exits, leaving* ANDY *in the ladies room. He looks at himself in the mirror, straightens his tie and hair.*)

ANDY: (*Counting, timing his exit*) 1-2-3-4-5-6-7-8-9-10. (*He exits the ladies room.*)

(*End of scene*)

Scene Four

(*Later, in an apartment with almost no furnishings except a small, cheap stereo playing music.* RACHEL *is very hung over.* ANDY *enters from the "kitchen" with a liquid in a glass, puts it down next to her.*)

RACHEL: Turn off this fucking music, okay?

(*He does*)

ANDY: Warm Coke.

RACHEL: Yum.

ANDY: It contains a patented formula that is an intestinal relaxant. You can buy the syrup from any local druggist. That's why pediatricians recommend it for children when they've got sick stomachs. Coca-Cola. Warm Coca-Cola.

RACHEL: How do you know these things?

ANDY: Feeling better—at all?

RACHEL: No.

ANDY: Sorry.

RACHEL: I feel like total shit.

ANDY: Yes.

(RACHEL *rummages in her purse, looking for her cigarettes.*)

RACHEL: I can smoke here, can't I? Isn't this where I'm staying?

ANDY: I'd prefer you didn't.

(RACHEL *looks at* ANDY.)

ANDY: The furniture's rented.

RACHEL: I won't burn anything.

ANDY: It's the smell.

RACHEL: You and I talk a lot about smells.

ANDY: Maybe that's because something stinks.

RACHEL: What?

ANDY: I think you should go ahead with this. Now, if you don't want to or if you're not up to it—fine. But it's the only way you can have any future at all. You're really, really smart and you have fucked up very, very badly. This is your chance to just step over the big pile of merde you have made of your life so far. And start over.

RACHEL: But she knows.

ANDY: Of course she knows. Everybody knows everything in this town.

RACHEL: Then what's the point?

ANDY: To confirm what we already know. If she has— becomes involved—with you, maybe there are or will

ACT ONE

be others. Other "contacts" are possible leaks, areas of vulnerability. And no one wants to go through that again.

RACHEL: Oh, but it was so much fun the last time. No need for anyone to even try to understand the real news, we had this dog stupid soap opera sucking up all the energy. No one needed to worry about the fact they couldn't even spell the names of places that were disappearing off the face of the earth because NO ONE was paying attention to—

ANDY: See? You do care.

RACHEL: I didn't think that was the question. The question is do I give a fuck about all this— this town and all the garbage postering.

ANDY: But this town is the hub of the world, Rachel. All those little circles that make up this city, and the streets extending out of them, like spokes of a wheel? Like the Nazca Plain with all those drawings of animals they thought were landing strips for aliens. Well, sometimes the map isn't the way to the secret— sometimes the map is the secret. Big wheels and little wheels—what goes around comes around. That's all it is.

RACHEL: No ideas.

ANDY: Just wheels.

RACHEL: That's bleak.

ANDY: That's the truth.

RACHEL: Internecine. Like that evil Italian family—the Medicis.

ANDY: Come on. We're just turning a few wheels ourselves. It's not like we're poisoning people.

RACHEL: Just the nation.

ANDY: What world do you live in? You're a criminal.

RACHEL: STOP SAYING I'M A CRIMINAL ALL THE TIME! I made a mistake.

ANDY: Yeah, you got caught.

RACHEL: I needed the money. It's not like it's habitual.

ANDY: You figured out a way to cheat at computer Dungeons and Dragons, when you were twelve. When you were fourteen, you rigged every game of "TEKRON" in Arlington, Virginia—so you could win. You took bets.

RACHEL: You had to get to Level Eight on your own and then, only then, could you go all the way with my shooting sequence. Anyone could have figured it out if they just watched carefully, but— *(Beat)* How did they know that? I never told anybody that. *You* didn't know that.

ANDY: No, but *we* know everything. Your bra size. The last time you had a bladder infection. The last time you bought Twinkies—at least if you bought them at the bigger grocery stores. And if we don't know it, we can find out.

RACHEL: You're scaring me.

ANDY: Good. Because I'm scared to death. At least I won't be alone in that.

RACHEL: Are there any sheets on the bed? I could sleep now.

ANDY: I'll make it up.

(ANDY *exits into the "bedroom."* RACHEL *looks around for her purse, finds her cigarettes, lights up. He rushes out to her, tries to grab the cigarette. She runs—he gives chase.)*

ANDY: The smoke alarm will go off!!!

RACHEL: Smoke alarms are impervious to cigarette smoke, Opie! But not to fire! Ha-ha!

ACT ONE

(To taunt ANDY, RACHEL *lifts her lighter up to the alarm. Nothing happens. Suddenly, they both become suspicious of the alarm. They go into an old problem-solving mode—two techno-brats faced with an anomaly. She lifts her cigarette lighter closer to the alarm. Nothing. He exits into the "kitchen", returns with a stool and a knife. While he's off, she sings into the alarm at the top of her lungs—to mock whatever "surveillance" is going on.)*

RACHEL: *(Sings)* Oh beautiful, for spacious skies!
For amber waves of grain!

ANDY: *(He returns with the stool, puts it down under the alarm and they both climb onto it and sing into the smoke alarm.)*
For purple mountains' majesty,
Above the fruited plain!

ANDY & RACHEL: *(Looking at each other)*
America! America!
God shed his grace on thee!
And crown thy good, with brotherhood—

(Some old emotions keep them from finishing this song. They just stand there next to each other for a beat, then RACHEL *gets down.)*

(Beat)

RACHEL: Such bullshit. We don't need some government biochip inserted into our craniums—we have years of school assemblies.

*(*RACHEL *gets the smoke alarm off the wall, hands it to* ANDY *who opens it and removes a small round object from it. She takes the object—the bug—to the light to see it better.)*

RACHEL: Oh, it's a really old bug—made in *America*. Who was the last person in this apartment? Nikita Krushchev?

ANDY: I'll finish making your bed.

RACHEL: No, I will, I will. I think I can bend over now without barfing.

ANDY: That's good.

RACHEL: I can drink, you know—I mean I haven't lost my ability to hold my liquor. I just haven't had any in such a long time. Other drugs—no problem. No booze. My favorite. Of course I couldn't get my favorite.

ANDY: It must have been tough. *(Beat)* No, I really mean that.

(Long silence between ANDY *and* RACHEL*)*

RACHEL: Do you want to stay the night? *(She answers her own questions quickly.)* No, if we're going to work together…
No, you've been drinking and there are rules about that.
No, I've seen you barf and, frankly, find you disgusting.
No, it's too late.
No, you're too fat.
No, you're a criminal and I'm a boy scout.
No, the fucking bed is probably bugged.
No, we might realize we knew each other in a previous lifetime.

(RACHEL *looks at* ANDY, *waiting to see if he will acknowledge this bit of truth. He turns away.)*

RACHEL: So you've re-made yourself completely, huh? Including rewriting our history.

ANDY: So we will be working together. Good. That's a good attitude.

RACHEL: You're a robot, aren't you?

ANDY: And you'll get a second chance at a decent life.

RACHEL: I have a decent life now. I'm out of prison.

ACT ONE

ANDY: You're on Supervised Release. Where will computer technology be by the time they let you near one again?

RACHEL: You're not a robot. You're a dick.

ANDY: Can you—for one second—stop listening to what you think I'm trying to do to you—and just consider the truth?

RACHEL: That seems to be such a slippery thing, particularly here.

ANDY: Don't try to leave.

RACHEL: I know.

ANDY: I'll see you in the morning.

(ANDY *leaves. We hear the door shut behind him.* RACHEL *picks up her pillow and exits into the "bedroom". The smoke alarm, now on the floor, goes off—she re-enters the room with her pillow, and puts it over the alarm, muting it—she picks up the knife and stabs the alarm several times. The alarm shuts off. He opens the door again, looks into the apartment.*)

RACHEL: I stabbed it. It's quiet now.

ANDY: Good. You did good. Goodnight.

(*He shuts the door. She stands for a minute, knife in hand. Then, repelled by it, flings it toward the kitchen.*)

RACHEL: Jesus!

(*End of scene*)

Scene Five

(ANDY *is in an elevator, going over a speech in a folder, making revisions.* JONI *enters dressed to the nines.*)

ANDY: Where's everyone else?

JONI: Don't wait for them.

(ANDY *pushes the button and the doors close, but the elevator doesn't move.* JONI *is looking at the speech now.*)

ANDY: I reincorporated those statistics Cal gave me on the way over and that quote we cut from the other speech.

JONI: Good.
So what did *you* think of the vote today?

ANDY: I'm sorry.

JONI: Ben and I had three issues and they killed each one. It just confirms what I've known all along—we're transitional, ideologically impotent. Fuck them.

ANDY: Is it safe in here?

JONI: Of course.

ANDY: What the hell was that? Coming into the ladies' room at the restaurant?

JONI: Do you blame me?

ANDY: Do you trust me?

JONI: You're not a spook, are you, Andy? Because I know they were talking to you after the campaign, before we brought you back on.

(ANDY *just shakes his head in disbelief.*)

ANDY: It's a little late to ask those kinds of questions.

JONI: I feel betrayed by the party. Ben and I have been sold out by some of our closest colleagues—just to be some sort of Band-aid on this gaping wound left by the previous administration.

ANDY: Is this elevator going to move? At all?

JONI: They have to check all the floors.

ANDY: Where's my tie?

JONI: *(Hands it to him)* You left it in the limo.

ACT ONE

(JONI *watches as* ANDY *puts it on, frantically. Beat*)

JONI: You're claustrophobic? How have you been able to stand all the enclosed spaces of your life?

ANDY: As long as I'm moving.

JONI: And, you'll move again, Andrew. And upwards.

ANDY: I don't care about that—I care about this issue.

JONI: And this is what I care about. You said you'd do anything for me.

ANDY: I meant it.

JONI: Because once we start this rolling, it will be just me and you.

ANDY: I think it is rolling. Isn't it?

JONI: Yeah.

ANDY: Because she thinks it's rolling.

JONI: It's rolling.

ANDY: *(Looking right at her)* I'm your Boy Scout.

JONI: I know. *(She straightens his tie perfunctorily.)* So, Andrew, I like thinking of it this way—we're setting a big, sort of, righteous fire that will attract all the cameras and writers, like moths.

ANDY: A big fire.

JONI: A twenty-one alarm fire.

ANDY: Why twenty-one?

JONI: That's how many guns they fire when they bury a president.

(Elevator dings.)

JONI: Okay, now we'll go very fast. It's one of the perks of the job.

(Elevator starts to move up.)

ANDY: Do I look all right?

JONI: Oh—you're not going in. That's not the media coverage I want. Ben isn't with me tonight, so I don't want to muddy the waters with you as an escort. Because it will probably appear in someone's monologue tomorrow night because none of them are smart enough to make a decent joke about what's really happening in the world. Oh, Mort Sahl, where are you? I miss you.

ANDY: Who?

(Beat, as JONI *sighs at the loss of another bit of her history.)*

JONI: Maybe it's time to just turn the world over to the next generation and let THEM fuck it up.

(Elevator dings. They've arrived at the floor.)

JONI: I was a LUG at Vasser, you know. Lesbian Until Graduation? It worked for me at the time.

*(*JONI *exits the elevator and walks into a bank of lights for camcorders. The elevator doors close and* ANDY *is sent downward at a very fast rate. It stops. And* ANDY *steps out of the elevator, takes out his cell phone and hits a number.)*

ANDY: *(Into cell phone)* I didn't find out anything we didn't already know. Later. *(He closes up the cell phone, pockets it, exits.)*

Scene Six

(Next morning, in the apartment. RACHEL *is on the phone)*

RACHEL: Mom? It's me. Is she home from school yet?
I said it's me. Is Jennifer home from school?
No, I'm…in D C.
Don't get upset—I'm not going to visit—it's just a training program of some kind.
Of course you can call them and check on it.
Don't hang up yet! Don't—!
She has Bible study—I forgot what day it was.

ACT ONE

Did she get the little skirt I ordered—?
Did she like it? What did she say when she opened it?
Say that again. *(She loves hearing the repetition.)*
That's good. That's good.
No, don't mention this training thing—I don't want to get her hopes up.
Well, all right—my hopes, then.
I know. I know it's not my day to call, but I miss talking to her so much.
I know, I know it upsets her. I know I have no right—
I know. I know everything, Mom.
I know I say that all the time.
I know I don't know everything.
Okayokayokay.
Right.
Yeah.
Tell—bye.
(She hangs up the phone. Looking toward the door)
Where the fuck is he? Where is he, goddammit!

(We hear someone's key in the door ANDY *enters with a bag containing a carton of orange juice and a newspaper.)*

RACHEL: Where've you been?

ANDY: Did you find some breakfast stuff in the refrigerator?

RACHEL: No.

ANDY: You've got a date at four P M.

RACHEL: With...her?

ANDY: Uh-huh.

RACHEL: *(Real panic)* Where? What am I going to wear? I look terrible!

ANDY: I knew you were a girl.

RACHEL: If I'm being dicked around again—if I'm a... pawn, a shrub in someone's big perverted garden, I swear, I'll kill the...gardener, the estate owner, and you. But you, you will go first.

ANDY: Oh, you are so tough. Isn't this where you call me "Bucko"?

(RACHEL *starts to hit* ANDY, *he grabs her wrists.*)

ANDY: You keep trying to get power in this situation. I appreciate that. I admire that. But, fact is, you have—no—power. Do you understand? And you can get no power.

RACHEL: Let go of me, you bastard prick.

ANDY: Of course. *(He lets go of her wrists.)* There's nothing you can tell the press that will mean anything. They'll use your story for whatever agenda they've got going at the moment. Hell, they could portray you as a spy for the tobacco industry! "Allegations" is the ticket for anyone grabbing power to say anything they want or need to say. Any information that you think you have that you want to leak to anyone, that person knows about it already. You see, it's hard to blackmail people in a society where anything goes—and is usually on the news twenty seconds later—and is forgotten on account of being topped by something even more bizarre by dinner time. You can call a lawyer, even. I believe you know some. And *he* will be playing, probably, *me* in the T V movie of all of this. *Or she, okay?*

RACHEL: *(Really intense, insistent)* If I'm ever to have custody of my daughter again—there can't be a T V movie—and everything will be in secret. You understand that.

ANDY: Of course.

RACHEL: And I won't be talking to a confidant with a weight problem, bad hair and a tape recorder. I won't

ACT ONE

talk to anybody. Nobody will talk to anybody. Got that?

ANDY: Of course. We have learned something from the past, you know.

RACHEL: No, we haven't. We never do. And that's why I assume there will be internal surveillance because there always is. They'll probably pass around the films for late-night viewing. Yuck! Yuck.

ANDY: There'll be no films.

RACHEL: Videotape. Digitally mastered images, whatever.

ANDY: No. All we will have is your word—your word about what happened, whether or not she's gay. And that's all we want.

RACHEL: Then why don't they just plant a... professional? There must be some—for women. I mean, women, for women.

ANDY: I'm sure you meant to say "sex worker."

RACHEL: Whatever.

ANDY: The sex industry is for straight men or gay men—it's not set up for women.

RACHEL: Yet.

ANDY: Oh, and this would be "liberation."

RACHEL: A woman should be able to pay for sex, just like a man—with money, not heartbreak.

ANDY: Exactly. And that's exactly why we need you. A gay woman might actually fall in love. And then emotions would be involved. Strong emotions. And you've got a situation that can go on for decades—think of the expose' books, the movies, the talk-show appearances, then the posters, tee-shirts, action figures. A gay woman in love with and then spurned by, arguably, the most powerful woman in the country—that woman would become a professional gay person. Ambassadoress of Gaydonia. And there's no guarantee that our Joan—Joni would go for this professional sex-worker spy type. She already likes you.

RACHEL: Action figures!!!!???

ANDY: It's a joke.

RACHEL: "Decades?"

ANDY: She'd also be set for life.

RACHEL: "Life?" Okay—I can't risk it—I want out.

ANDY: Sure?

RACHEL: Yes.

ANDY: Okay.

RACHEL: Okay. *(Beat)* What happens now?

ANDY: You go back on a technical violation.

RACHEL: Of what?

ANDY: Of Supervised Release—you snorted coke in the ladies' room of La Ferme. You can be "skiing" with your "roommate" in a few hours.

RACHEL: How did you know all that now? And I only told her about my roommate.

ANDY: Her? Joan?

RACHEL: Yeah.

ANDY: And you don't want to do this? You've already confided in her. There's already a connection.

RACHEL: I'm not scamming her because she already knows. And I'm not scamming you because you hired me to scam her. I'm not even a good dyke. So what good am I to anyone?

ANDY: You suffer from low self-esteem.

ACT ONE 25

RACHEL: Why did you choose me?

ANDY: You're really smart. You're really beautiful. And I know you.

RACHEL: But do you, Andy? Know me? Really? And did you ever? Other than in the Biblical sense?

ANDY: You dumped me.

RACHEL: I didn't dump you. We had one argument. You never called.

ANDY: You told me to go fuck myself and read some Greek drama, specifically, Oedipus, as if I didn't know what that comment was about, and to leave you alone!! I mean, Rachel—Jesus!— *(Silence)* Look—we were young and then I got that internship and—and—you were too fucking intense for me! Okay? Does that surprise you??

RACHEL: No.

ANDY: You—you are so smart but you are so dumb at the same time!

RACHEL: I just don't like to be dicked around!!!

ANDY: It was years ago!

RACHEL: I'm not talking about then. I mean NOW! That was two seconds ago—we covered that. I've moved on! You are so slow. I'm saying I value freedom! I value choice! Particularly after the last three years! Does that surprise you??!

ANDY: You have a choice. You can choose to change your life. How difficult will the job be really? It's completely professional—clean. No emotions. You're there. You participate however you need to…you report back to me. We pay you. A lot. You get your child back because you'll have a life to raise her in.

RACHEL: But it can never be said that I'm gay. I'll never get my daughter back from my mother, as a criminal who's also a gay woman.

ANDY: You could fight that and in a good world, a world of the, I hope, not so far future, it wouldn't be an issue. But you won't have to fight it. Okay? Can we go shopping now? *(Hands her one of the cups of liquid he brought)* Here. You should have some of this O J—vitamin C. I don't want you getting a cold. Or giving one to somebody.
Drink it.
I'll wait.

(ANDY *takes out the newspaper, starts to read it.* RACHEL *opens the orange juice and takes a drink directly from the carton.)*

RACHEL: I'm in a big video game and someone's got the controller, but I'll figure it out. You know that, don't you? Don't you?

ANDY: Paranoia—low self-esteem breeds it. They go hand-in-hand, like co-dependent lovers.

RACHEL: And if you ever grab me again, I'll kill you.

(End of scene)

Scene Seven

(Gym. JONI *is in workout clothes and exercising with a vengeance—some of it with weights.)*

MAN'S VOICE: *(Ben's, on the P A)* Joni? Joni?

(JONI *pauses, but goes back to arm curls.)*

MAN'S VOICE: Joni? Are you in there?

(JONI *keeps exercising.)*

ACT ONE

MAN'S VOICE: You have to eat dinner alone again. Sorry. I told the kitchen.

(JONI *stops.*)

MAN'S VOICE: I love you, Sweetheart. See you later, okay?

(JONI *sinks to her knees, defeated. Lights down.*)

(End of scene)

Scene Eight

(*Lights up.* JONI *is sitting, holding the weights, sweaty, with a towel around her neck.* ANDY *enters.*)

JONI: Is he gone?

ANDY: Yes.

JONI: We've always had an honest relationship—but I don't tell him everything. I can't tell him this—yet.

ANDY: Of course you can't.

RACHEL: We've been equal partners—he and I. It's been a great…partnership. (*The import of everything gets to her for a moment.*) Oh man.

ANDY: Yes.

JONI: So I've been thinking and I do like her.

ANDY: I do, too.

JONI: She's nice.

ANDY: I agree.

JONI: And smart.

ANDY: Oh yeah.

JONI: How much trouble was she in?

ANDY: A lot.

JONI: And we're rehabilitating her. And they say this administration hasn't done enough at home. It's a domestic project. For me. Retraining for the female ex-con. Lovely.

ANDY: Yes, it is.

JONI: This will help her, though, won't it?

ANDY: Of course.

JONI: So you do get the "do-gooder" prize—you have plumbed the depths—did I say "depths"? I meant "heights" of "do-gooderism."

ANDY: Thanks.

JONI: But Andy, for incendiary tabloid headline potential and, most importantly, the moral mooning of this Congress, you, baby, get my life-long admiration.

ANDY: And...her mother's a Baptist.

JONI: No.

ANDY: A serious one. Yeah.

JONI: The child of one of their own. They'll come after me and try to smite me good. Brilliant.

ANDY: Thank you.

JONI: And that's a nice tie.

ANDY: Been shopping. For her. So I got something for myself. She picked it out.

JONI: I wondered. Doesn't look like you. I mean, your taste. Looks good, though.

ANDY: She attacked me this morning— *(Quickly)* I mean, verbally, in anger. She's...not an easy person, you know.

JONI: I don't care what happens between the two of you.

ANDY: I think she'd like to beat me up.

ACT ONE

JONI: You are a strange dude.

ANDY: Women make generalizations about me all the time and I'm sick of it. No matter what I do—I always need to be doing something different.

JONI: Change the world or just change yourself and let it roll. I've been modified so many times, I have stretch marks on my psyche. From the time I was born, it seems I've always needed to be modified.

ANDY: Not to me.

(She turns around and really looks at him.)

JONI: Andrew, Andrew. You've been a handmaiden so long, you don't know what you think. I know from worn knees and rug burns. Okay? I have my share. And we both know I'm not talking about sex. Sometime, before you die or retire, you need to find your soul and get it back into your body. I don't know when it took flight, but it flew away for sure. On the Beltway, I see pieces of black plastic garbage bags hung up in the bare tree limbs and I think, "That's what so-and-so's soul looks like now because he or she never retrieved it." But yours—it's somewhere, looking like a little bird that's stopped thrashing and is just hanging there, waiting. But at least it's still alive.

ANDY: They'd think it was funny—us talking about souls.

JONI: Who? Oh, you mean the Christian right. Yeah, they've tried to pretty much dominate the definition of the word. The irony is that ever since I decided to take them on, head-to-head, on this issue, I've felt like I was getting my soul back. You know, like it was coming back to me. Because the issue, Andy—the issue is what I'm thinking about all the time now. Promising to make this one change and not caring if it brings me down.

ANDY: All right, then. Let's begin. But before we do this irrevocable thing, I have to say this: Why? We worked so hard. Who cares about promises—campaign or personal. Don't you realize? You're here. You got elected. You're the promise—you're the biggest promise in history!

JONI: And that's the problem, goddamit!! What I've done or haven't done has never, for a minute, mattered more than the simple fact that I got elected! I'm the first. Period. Or, I should say, I'm the first with a period. Oh, the estrogen and menopause jokes have never quit. I hated that right-wing cunt Margaret Thatcher, but, in the last three years, I've developed a real sympathy for her. I mean, surely you realize, Andy, that I was nominated because my life was considered to be cleaner and more boring than David Souter's. They didn't want to run a nun, so they got me—a school marmish New England Senator who's devoted to her husband. I talked the talk, I had the right ideas, and I wasn't going to stray from the political or sexual path. Then the public went to the polls and voted for this newly created Giant Mom, and so it came to pass that dead-from-the-waist-down June Cleaver moved into the White House.

ANDY: So all this is just revenge?

JONI: No, it's revanche. As in taking back territory.

ANDY: What territory?

JONI: Moral territory.
Didn't you ever look at our opponent—didn't you ever look at the religious right some time and think, "if only I could see the world that simply, I could put all my energies into giving everything to this one right thing." Why do liberals have to be mired in complexities and gray areas all the time? I've started to feel that way again. Civil rights. Ending the War in

ACT ONE   31

Viet-Nam. Those issues were clear. That clarity. That passion. I haven't had passion in my life in such a long time. It's consuming me and it's wonderful. You think I'm having some kind of menopausal psychotic breakdown, don't you?

ANDY: No.

JONI: You're lying.

ANDY: A little.

JONI: Well, that's a beginning. Catch.

(JONI *throws the weights to* ANDY—*he catches them. She exits. He puts them down carefully and exits.*)

(End of scene)

Scene Nine

(RACHEL *is outdoors in a beautiful, sylvan setting. She is dressed in "woodsy" clothes—brand new. She lights up a cigarette. After a beat,* JONI *enters, dressed as if she's been jogging or doing a power walk.*)

RACHEL: Wo! *(She puts out the cigarette)* Hi. They made me walk here alone.

JONI: You're not alone.

RACHEL: No, you're here.

JONI: Everyone is here. Everyone is everywhere. Always.

(RACHEL *looks around.*)

RACHEL: I won't get Lyme disease, will I? I mean, wooded areas are supposed to be infested with deer ticks.

JONI: You're not an outdoors person at all, are you?

RACHEL: No. But it's a real concern. People have been getting very sick. It lasts your whole life. It's crippling.

JONI: I'm Joni.

RACHEL: I know. We met in the john at that French restaurant.

JONI: It's really pretentious, that place.

RACHEL: Yeah. And what's with the dill sauce? Tasted like... *(Beat)* What are we doing?

JONI: We're dating.
Relax.
All you have to do is just be—

RACHEL: Myself?

JONI: My girlfriend.

RACHEL: Man, do I need a cigarette.

JONI: Go ahead. Just as long as you don't ignite the woods.

(RACHEL *lights up.*)

RACHEL: This won't bother you, will it?

JONI: No.

RACHEL: Because I can control it.

JONI: Can you?

RACHEL: I mean, I don't have to smoke.

JONI: You don't?

RACHEL: Have you ever been a therapist?

JONI: Do I sound like one?

RACHEL: Do you?

JONI: I don't know—what do you think?

(They both laugh. Then suddenly, RACHEL *freezes in fear and then goes nuts—she feels a tick on her neck and tries to get it off.)*

ACT ONE

RACHEL: Can you see it?!

JONI: *(Getting her to sit so she can examine her.)* No, no. You still feel it?

RACHEL: I don't think so.

(Another itch—RACHEL freaks.)

JONI: Just...let me look. *(She examines RACHEL's neck and hair, gently.)* Calm down. You're fine. You're...fine.

(RACHEL calms down. JONI notices the label on the collar.)

JONI: This is a quality shirt.

RACHEL: I have some beautiful outfits now, and I'd just like to thank whoever paid for them. And shoes. I never had really fine shoes before. Girl shoes. I was looking in the mirror, and I thought, "I look pretty good."

JONI: Yeah.

RACHEL: Oh, I didn't mean—I mean, that wasn't—you know—said with a purpose.

JONI: I know. That's what I like about you.

RACHEL: You do?

JONI: You're ingenuous. No agenda.

RACHEL: ...Yeah.

JONI: Let's sit down.

(They sit.)

RACHEL: It's beautiful here. So many famous people, world leaders, not to mention all the Presidents and Russians and—

JONI: Spies?

RACHEL: I've kind of lost track of what I'm supposed to know. Can you explain it to me?

JONI: Could you be the one relationship in my life where I don't have to do that?

RACHEL: Yeah.

JONI: Just trust me.

RACHEL: Okay.

JONI: You can.

(Beat)

RACHEL: Cool.
Thank you for the clothes.

JONI: No problem.

RACHEL: Can I ask a question?

JONI: As long as it doesn't require an executive answer of any kind.

RACHEL: I don't think it does.
Has there ever been a, you know, gay President?

JONI: You mean after Eleanor Roosevelt?

(They both laugh.)

RACHEL: And she was…?

JONI: F D R's wife.

RACHEL: *(Not sure, still, but covers it)* Oh, yeah.

(Beat)

JONI: Are you asking if I'm gay?

RACHEL: Yeah.

JONI: I kissed you in the john—what do you think?

RACHEL: I think you're a good kisser.

JONI: You want me to make your job easy, huh?

RACHEL: What is my…job now? I really want to do it, whatever it is. I don't have fixed ideas about sexuality and I've slept with women. And enjoyed it. With drugs. I didn't mean, I needed the drugs to enjoy women, I just meant those-times-I-had-sex-with-women, I was, you know, stoned. *(Beat)* I mean, I think sexual identity is about who you can fall in love with, and I've just never, you know, been in love with a woman. *(Beat)* I fall in love with men. I hate the motherfuckers. But I fall in love with them.

JONI: Me, too.

RACHEL: *(Surprised)* Which part?

JONI: Men.

RACHEL: You hate them?

JONI: No. No, most of my friends are men. I prefer them to women. As friends.

RACHEL: Why?

(Beat. JONI is taken back by the question.)

JONI: I don't know.
You know, this is the first time I've ever really wanted to answer that question, and I don't know the answer.

RACHEL: *(Sits back down)* I have a lot of women friends—well, events have somewhat dictated the gender of my current friends. I really like my… roommate. Thank god. She's not violent, fucked up. They don't have to come in at two A M to give her her anti-psychotic medicine.

JONI: But she's a coke head. *(Seeing that RACHEL is suspicious of how she knows this)* You said—intimated—in the ladies' room—where we met.

RACHEL: Yeah…Yeah. *(Beat)* Everyone's addicted—to something. Right?

JONI: What are you addicted to?

RACHEL: They won't let me near a computer.

JONI: What do you do instead?

RACHEL: Play cards. Games. Go mad.
Can I have a computer? In the apartment?

JONI: Never happen. Your record. Even I'm answerable to the justice system.

RACHEL: I thought you could do anything.

JONI: Watch any news at all in the last few years?

RACHEL: Well, yeah. I just—

JONI: If I had that kind of power, this world would be a very different place.

RACHEL: What would be different?

JONI: I have a long list.

RACHEL: What's at the top?

JONI: Justice. Real justice.

RACHEL: Justice. Not love?

JONI: Eva Braun loved Hitler. Mussolini loved his mistress, very much, in fact. They died together.

RACHEL: But "love is all you need."

JONI: If you're the Beatles.

RACHEL: Yeah, but doesn't love bring everything else.

JONI: No.
Isn't it obvious it doesn't?

RACHEL: But if you love somebody, you want to be Just—in the sense of justice—with them. Right?

JONI: Do you? Abraham and Isaac, for example?

RACHEL: Yeah, but those Biblical people were so fucked up. Besides, I meant "in love."

JONI: That's the worse kind. Ever hear of crimes of passion?

RACHEL: You were a lawyer, weren't you?

ACT ONE

JONI: In a previous life. When I had one. You're adorable.

RACHEL: Thanks.

JONI: Don't worry.

RACHEL: I'm not.

(They hear a twig crack.)

JONI: Let's see if we can ditch them.

RACHEL: Really?

JONI: Yeah.
Follow me—and watch for the branches.

(JONI grabs RACHEL's hand and they run off into the "woods". After a beat, ANDY enters, still in his suit, and looks around for them, then looks at his watch.)

ANDY: Right. *(He exits the way he came.)*

(End of scene)

Scene Ten

(Night. ANDY is sitting in one of the back seats of a very nice van—lots of comfort and low light. The engine is on. He has his cell phone up to his ear, listening intently to someone talking to him on the line. Suddenly, he cuts off the call, and pockets the cell phone. JONI climbs into the van and sits next to him. She's still in her outdoor clothes, but very disheveled, with a few marks on her skin.)

ANDY: She's here. *(Shuts off cell phone)* Okay?

JONI: Yep.

ANDY: You're awesome.

JONI: Maybe.

ANDY: She's—

JONI: Gone. Taken care of.

ANDY: *(To a driver we don't see)* Let's roll.

JONI: Shut the door.

ANDY: Right.

(He shuts the van door from the inside. Lights go out on them. Sound of van driving off into the night)

(End of scene)

Scene Eleven

(ANDY turns on a light—he's standing, loosening his tie, talking into his cell phone [To Ben].)

ANDY: Ben? Sorry, it took me this long to get back.
Yeah, it's a done deal now—she went all the way.
I've done what I can do.
Not until morning.
No, no I'm here. Where else would I be?
Right.
(He turns off the cell phone, closes his eyes, almost falls asleep on his feet, comes to, then shakes himself awake and walks off.)

(End of scene)

Scene Twelve

(Dark interior. Lots of crashing and rummaging around. Then silence. Suddenly, a small flame is seen. It's a cigarette lighter and touches the end of a cigarette. Someone takes a long drag and emits a deeply satisfied sigh. Then the sound of a bit more rummaging and a lamp comes on, illuminating RACHEL, sitting and smoking on the floor of the living room of the apartment, in disarray. Her face and arms are scratched from the run in the woods. Knock at the door)

RACHEL: Yeah?

ACT ONE 39

ANDY: *(Unseen, other side of door)* Andy.

RACHEL: Yeah?

ANDY: *(Unseen, other side of door)* Bucko.

RACHEL: Okay.

(RACHEL *opens the door.* ANDY *walks in—dressed in some unlikely and almost outrageous, for him, casual garb—with shades on.)*

RACHEL: Okay—who was that dork in the van? Huh? And what was with all those photographers!!! We were supposed to be in a controlled situation. That you were, supposedly, controlling. I think we're getting away—big fun—running in the woods—freedom—whatever—LYME TICK INFESTED WOODS—and whammo!!! Flashes everywhere! I felt like Madonna and I DIDN'T LIKE IT!!! So now—NOW—my face is plastered all over magazines that MY BAPTIST, RIGHT-WING MOTHER WILL SEE AS SHE STANDS IN LINE AT THE GROCERY STORE!!!!

ANDY: But you're not gay, right? You're working for me.

RACHEL: You?

ANDY: The…government.

RACHEL: BUT MY MOTHER DOESN'T KNOW THAT!!!

ANDY: Yes, she does.
Call her.

RACHEL: I tried—she wasn't—

ANDY: She is now. I just talked to her.

(RACHEL *dials the number. Waits only a beat or two. Gets her mother on the line)*

RACHEL: Hi…
Right. It's me.

No, I'm fine.
That's what he said.
Yeah. It's a great opportunity.
No, I don't have to carry a gun—there's no danger, really.
No, she's not stuck-up, Mother. She's nice. I like her.
Yes, she has her own hair dresser.
How is—
She hasn't seen the news or anything, has she?
You tell her—tell her—that what they're saying isn't true. And it isn't, Mom.
Oh, you have. Oh.
Thanks.
Thanks.

Tell her I love her. Hug her for me.
Okay.
(She hangs up the phone, amazed.)
That's the nicest she's ever been to me. Ever.

ANDY: I told her you were being trained as a bodyguard—

RACHEL: That explains the "gun" remark.

ANDY: —and that you'll be introduced to the public as that very soon.

RACHEL: She said she was proud of me. She's never been proud of me.
She said that she explained it all to Jennifer.
And Jennifer understands what I'm doing.

ANDY: So, everything's all right now. See?

RACHEL: Maybe—it's so hard to trust it.
Things have been bad for so long.

ANDY: Trust it.

RACHEL: Things have never been all right. For me. Before.

ACT ONE 41

ANDY: Then it's time.

(Beat)

RACHEL: Will I get to eat in this new life?

ANDY: I'm taking you out. But we have to be careful. If they find out you're here, I'll have to find another place for you to live.

RACHEL: What difference does it make?

ANDY: Rachel, we have to control the situation. Everything has gone according to plan. And it's been good, right? So I ducked the press with my disguise.

RACHEL: Disguise.

ANDY: I'm unrecognizable outside of my suit.

RACHEL: That's sad.

ANDY: Just get dressed and I'll take you wherever you want to eat.

RACHEL: I'd bag those shades, entirely—yikes.

(He does. She exits into the "bedroom".)

RACHEL: I want to eat at Denny's.

ANDY: Missing prison food?

RACHEL: *(From the "bedroom" as she's getting dressed)* They've got a smoking section.
All these nice clothes and no place to wear them.

ANDY: Their time will come. *(He starts to clean up the disarray left from RACHEL's earlier rummaging in the dark.)* God, what happened in here?

RACHEL: Sorry. I live here right? Are you cleaning up?

ANDY: No.

(RACHEL enters from the "bedroom", dressed casually but nicely.)

ANDY: You look nice.

RACHEL: I feel so good. It's a new thing—a brand new thing. *(She crosses to window.)* They're not really out there—

ANDY: Get away from the window!

RACHEL: You're so *noir*.

ANDY: If they see you we'll get mobbed!

RACHEL: How can we leave?

ANDY: By the freight elevator.

RACHEL: Just one look.

(ANDY *grabs her.* RACHEL *downs him with an instinctive protective response, a hit in the nuts. He's on the floor, stunned with pain.*)

RACHEL: I told you NOT to ever grab me! *(Rubbing her arm where he grabbed her)* Ow. *(Examines her upper arm)* I'm probably going to have a bruise. *(To* ANDY, *on the floor)* Try to breathe. You're holding your breath. That's bad.

ANDY: *(Constricted)* Oh my god.

RACHEL: Never happened to you before? I am surprised.

(RACHEL *helps* ANDY *up—he tries to breathe and stand.*)

ANDY: Wo.

(RACHEL *puts out her hand to shake.*)

RACHEL: Still friends?

ANDY: I don't know.

RACHEL: Hey, come on. If I were a guy, we'd be buying each other drinks.

ANDY: If you were a guy, I'd of clocked you.

RACHEL: When? Now—that you can breathe again and stand up?

ANDY: *(About the punch)* Where did you learn that?

RACHEL: Your first shot should always be your best. You may not get another one, especially if you're female. I'm surprised your mother didn't teach you any of this or don't they cover that in feminist theory?

ANDY: Your anger at me is—is—

RACHEL: Is what?

ANDY: You refuse to see beyond these old…I'm not some stereotypical, male—

RACHEL: Asshole? No, no, clearly, you're a newer, gentler goon. You know—I just have to say this—for someone who is actually participating in a form of fag bashing—I mean, that's what surveillance and entrapment are—EVEN WHEN THE SUBJECT KNOWS SHE'S BEING SPIED ON—you're awfully sensitive for a thug.

ANDY: You can abuse me, whatever, but I'm not going to let you ruin this for yourself. No matter how hard you try.

RACHEL: Oh, so I try to fuck up my life. That must be the problem. Thanks for clearing that up—I wondered why my life was in the shithole. I was trying to go to prison.

ANDY: What were you trying to do?

RACHEL: Make a life for myself. And Jennifer. And I did for three years.

ANDY: Until you got busted and sent away for three years. That is half of your daughter's life.
How old is she?
She's six, right?
She's six.

(Long beat)

RACHEL: Oh! You think she's yours?! She's not yours. Is that why you did all this? Well, you're off the hook. After you've nearly destroyed our lives, you can go!

ANDY: Look, Rachel! I got you an early out. I got you a job. I'm trying to fix things, so you can have—and she—can have security and a future.

RACHEL: She's not yours!!!
You weren't the only man in my life, you arrogant prick!
I went to a bar. I picked some guy up! And then there was—whathisname—Jim.

ANDY: I'll try to arrange a blood test as soon—

RACHEL: Look, I don't fucking need you!! I never did! See? So stop all this fucking "trying".

(Beat. He waits for the emotion to die down—his and hers.)

ANDY: This is America. The land of opportunity. I get to try.
At least. I get to try.
Right? Right?

(RACHEL *doesn't answer. Resigned and recovered from the pain, he checks his watch.*)

ANDY: Let's go—I want to watch something on T V in an hour or so.

(RACHEL *looks at* ANDY.)

ANDY: Basketball game. I'm a guy! Okay? Can't I just be a simple fucking guy for five fucking minutes?

(ANDY *escorts* RACHEL *out the door.*)

(End of scene)

Scene Thirteen

ACT ONE 45

(In the blackout, we hear JONI's *voice coming from a television.)*

JONI: Thank you all for coming. Before I take any questions on the meetings my husband and I attended in Riga on the impending ecological disaster in Southern Russia and Latvia, I'd like to make this statement: I have been an American since my birth, fifty one years ago. When I entered the political arena, I expected my life and the life of my spouse to be open to public scrutiny. Even after the absurd level of reportage of the private lives of public figures in the past, I don't think anyone thought the practice would change, and it didn't. My past and the past of my spouse—

(Inside a room for news briefing. We just see the podium with JONI *there, talking into the microphones. Lots of flashes from everywhere. She is dressed very nicely, conservatively, but pretty and feminine with make-up and a nice coif. On her face and arms, we can see a couple of marks from the branches she and* RACHEL *hit as they ran through the woods.)*

JONI: —have been plundered for every detail that could be judged. Intimate details of our childhoods, our adolescence, our courtship and marriage were chronicled each night on the news as you ate your dinner. Old boyfriends, girlfriends, employers and any family member who would appear on television were interviewed. Our college transcripts were printed on posters. Painful details of our lives were discussed by hostile and wise-cracking talk-show hosts. Both of us developed tremendous compassion for families involved in brutal tragedies because we knew how it felt to hear your life chronicled, often incorrectly, as we went about our day. However, we also knew that we hadn't been the victim of a terrible tragedy at all—in fact, we were the victims of an incredible privilege—

the privilege to serve the greatest democracy the world has seen. After a long and exhausting campaign, to our great joy, neither of us were found wanting—with all the thorough scrutiny, we passed the test. When we took office—and I say "we" because, in fact, though you only elected one of us, both of us have been serving this great country at least eighteen out of every twenty-four hours—when we took office, you heard the oath that every person in that high office has spoken since George Washington. That oath has been kept. As the first woman to hold this office, I would like to make this point very clear—in the best tradition of Roe versus Wade—my body belongs to me and that includes my feelings of passion and love. And now we'll return to the questions on the Latvian conference.

(Someone from the audience—Sam Donaldson-sounding voice—shouts a question.)

VOICEOVER: *(Sam Donaldson voice or actual audience plant)* Madam President. You were seen emerging from the woods around Camp David with a young woman. You were both flushed and flustered. Who is she?

JONI: The ecology of Latvia has been nearly destroyed by the environmental irresponsibility of the once Soviet Union and the current Russian Republic's inability to provide an infrastructure to deal with the ever-escalating and devastating ecological problems. Latvia's water resources— *(She stops and looks out at the crowd.)* I might be in love with her. It's a little early. I'm sure you all understand—I'm sure you've all been there. Some of you are probably there right now. We haven't had sex yet—by any definition, and I don't want to rush that. Her name is Rachel. She's a real smart, nice, funny, attractive person. Oh, and Sam? That's spelled L-E-S-B-I-A-N.

ACT ONE

(Lots of flashes of photographs and pandemonium of people yelling, "Madam President! Madam President!" Lights then come up on ANDY, *standing in the apartment, with his coat still on, having just come back from eating. He is staring at the television—and is seeing what the audience sees live on stage—*JONI *smiling and trying to get away from the questions and lights of the news reporters.* ANDY *is beaming.* RACHEL *enters, in her coat.)*

ANDY: *(To the television)* Yes! Let the future start now!

(RACHEL *listens to the television for a beat.)*

ANDY: Rachel, it's an amazing day—

RACHEL: YOU FUCKING JERK!!!! YOU NAZI!!!!!

ANDY: Don't you see? The ball is in the basket!!!

RACHEL: HOW COULD YOU DO THIS TO YOUR OWN CHILD?????!! I'LL NEVER GET HER BACK NOW!!!!

(But ANDY *doesn't move his eyes off the image of* JONI *on the television.* RACHEL *grabs her purse and escapes out the door—he doesn't seem to see her go.)*

ANDY: I love this game. I LOVE THIS GAME!

*(*ANDY *turns around and sees that* RACHEL's *gone. He turns off the TV with the remote control, sits down on the couch. On his face we see the pain of what all this is costing him.)*

ANDY: Right.

END OF ACT ONE

ACT TWO

Scene One

(JONI *is in a garden. She's trimming the flowers she's picked—all for a photo op, and not doing a good job.* ANDY *arrives—she hands him the basket with the picked but untrimmed flowers.*)

ANDY: Have you ever done this before?

(JONI *gives* ANDY *a look.*)

ANDY: I mean, this looks good—you in the garden—for the press.

JONI: Snipping these flowers keeps me from snipping your balls off. I've got a breakfast meeting in ten minutes and I've been out here farting around with these stupid flowers.

ANDY: I can control her.

JONI: Starting when?

ANDY: I know exactly what I'm doing.

JONI: Tell me. I thought she was a completely willing player.

ANDY: I know where she's gone. She's gone to see her daughter. It'll add to the story.

JONI: She's our worst fear—a loose cannon. Or—since I declared my "love" for her on national television—a nuclear warhead on…a skateboard.

ANDY: But you do like her.

JONI: You're standing here sounding like a Yenta, while she's out there talking to god knows who, making me look like some Machiavellian monster!

ANDY: She's not doing that. I know it.

JONI: Look. We need to re-orient ourselves. What are we doing? We are trying to platform an issue by creating a media firestorm. But wouldn't you agree that we need to control said storm or it will destroy everything I'm burning my political career to a crisp to accomplish!

ANDY: But this will help your career—in the long run.

JONI: How long? After I'm dead? Dead leaders are always the best—we love them.

ANDY: No, I'm serious. You'll come out on top.

JONI: How could you work in this town this long and be that optimistic?

ANDY: I believe people can change. I think it's possible. And I believe in what women can do.

JONI: Andy, you don't have to con me. Just do your job!

ANDY: *(Looking at his watch)* I ordered a car. It's just in Northern Virginia. And it's Sunday.

JONI: Just fix it. I'm alone here. I can't bring in the spin doctors because, like the real doctors they are, they demand the truth, the whole truth, and nothing but the truth. And I can't tell them that. Because all truth, even when it's false, gets out. Hand me the fucking flowers and go!

(ANDY *hands* JONI *the flowers and exits.*)

JONI: *(To someone offstage, but nearby)* Ben? Ben? I don't trust him any more. What's his other agenda? Because

ACT TWO

I know he's got one... *(She exits in the direction she was talking.)*

(End of scene)

Scene Two

(RACHEL is standing. Sound of a Baptist service going on [An unseen preacher reads from the Bible and quotes a psalm—very low]. After a beat or two, ANDY enters, comes up next to her.)

ANDY: Don't take off. Okay?

(RACHEL starts to leave, but ANDY holds her arm—not wanting to make a scene, she stays.)

RACHEL: I could kill you. And would, if I had a weapon.

ANDY: This child should and will be with her mother. I promise.

RACHEL: *(Incredulous)* You promise!?

ANDY: *(Noticing the congregation)* We're being stared at.

RACHEL: I don't want to have to leave. I don't know when I'll get to see her again. So you have to leave. Let go of me.

(ANDY does.)

ANDY: Can I just—for a moment—could I—where is she?

RACHEL: Up front. Next to my mother.

(ANDY strains to see.)

ANDY: Which one is your mother?

RACHEL: Don't call attention to yourself. Please go.

ANDY: I can't go. I'm not leaving until you believe that everything's going to be all right. *(Beat)* What's the message today?

RACHEL: The same one as always: Jesus died for our sins.

ANDY: Does that include mine?

RACHEL: Jesus was a better man than I am.

ANDY: Rachel, all of this—all of this—will come out fine. You have to believe me.

RACHEL: I trusted you. And I trusted the President of the United States. I am a complete idiot.

ANDY: Right now the press is working on you. With every word they write, you gain a constituency. And you're not even running for office. It's the Other American Currency, Rachel—influence.

RACHEL: Then why am I back here behind the "extra seats"? She won't even let me talk to her.

ANDY: I want to just look at her once. Where is she?

RACHEL: Up there—next to the witch. She's wearing a big pink barrette shaped like a bow—

(ANDY *strains to look, sees her, then looks down quickly and just breathes for a few beats.*)

ANDY: Oh my god.

RACHEL: Yeah. She's real. And smart, too.

ANDY: Oh my god.

RACHEL: Yeah.

(ANDY *looks again, really seeing his little girl.* RACHEL *just watches him.*)

ANDY: She's small for seven—

RACHEL: Six. She's six.
Mom brought her to see me twice. She hated it, of

ACT TWO 53

course. It upset her. So Mom said "no more" and that's the way it's been.

ANDY: The old lady looks reallllly old. And really mean. Does she treat her...I mean, should she be with her?

RACHEL: *(Staring at him incredulously)* You are...the limit.

ANDY: I'm sorry. I'm not thinking as clearly as I— How mean is she?

RACHEL: Only to me. And she doesn't mean to be mean—she's just...wrong.

ANDY: You called her "the witch."

RACHEL: She's my mother.

ANDY: Why can't you just go up there...

RACHEL: Why don't you take out a gun, hold the entire congregation hostage, and kidnap my mother and my daughter for me? You're so good at fixing things. You're so good at wielding power.

ANDY: You have every right to be angry with me.

RACHEL: You are the most insensitive, self- serving prick—

ANDY: Why won't you believe me? I did this all for you, Rachel. To give you an opportunity—

RACHEL: Oh, you are definitely Martin Luther King.

ANDY: You think it's easy for me...

RACHEL: Things have always been easy for you, Andy.

ANDY: That is not true.
It's not easy being here—I've never seen her.

RACHEL: Whose fault is that?

ANDY: Good question.
But we have to go. People are staring at us.

RACHEL: Noooo.

ANDY: We have to go.

RACHEL: Not yet.

ANDY: If there's a scene here, it won't help anything.

RACHEL: I just want to look at her a little longer.

ANDY: Rachel, trust me. I promise—everything will be all right.

RACHEL: That's what you said to me that night.

ANDY: Which night?

RACHEL: The night she was conceived—in the lounge of the computer center.

ANDY: You know which night?

RACHEL: It was the last night.

ANDY: Oh.
Trust me. Anyway.

RACHEL: Are you kidding?

ANDY: Trust me?

RACHEL: I can't.

ANDY: You have to.

RACHEL: Oh god…God help me.
Come on—it's getting to be that time in the service when people start to come forward—

ANDY: We could go up there and get closer?

RACHEL: Only if you want to be baptized.

ANDY: What?

RACHEL: If you go up there and present yourself—they have to take you in. They have to accept you. Because you're standing before god and them. Everything they believe in is there at that moment. You come just as you are and they HAVE TO take you. So, go up there,

ACT TWO 55

Andy, and have your sins washed away. We can go hand-in-hand, if you like—they can't deny us.

ANDY: If I do this—will you finally forgive me for everything I've done, haven't done, wanted to do, but fucked up, everything you're mad at me about, whether I'm guilty or not—

RACHEL: I'm not god.

ANDY: I'm not guilty.

RACHEL: I know.

(ANDY *tries to take* RACHEL *by the hand to leave, but she resists, but with one last look at their daughter, exits with him.*)

(End of scene)

Scene Three

(Sound of VOICES *on a television talk-show)*

VOICE ONE: I don't know if history repeats itself all the time or not. I don't know if that's true. When ever has there been a world leader who is homosexual and out, as they say?

VOICE TWO: One of those French kings wore a dress and was definitely out and everyone knew it.

VOICE THREE: Which French king?

VOICE FOUR: Oh, all of them, probably.

VOICE ONE: But adultery is—

VOICE FOUR: —the national pasttime. Big yawn.

VOICE TWO: But a female as the perpetrator—

VOICE THREE: "Perpetrator?" "Perpetrator?" What is this? Some cop program? Adultery's not a crime.

VOICE ONE: No, it's a commandment. Didn't we get clear on that a few years ago?

VOICE TWO: Wait a minute. To do it or not to do it?

VOICE ONE: You know what I mean.

VOICE FOUR: He or SHE who is without sin...

VOICE THREE: Put down that stone, Cokie.

VOICE FOUR: But they're not doing it yet—she said so.

VOICE THREE: I think they all cancel each other out and we need to move on.

VOICE TWO: But to what? To what? Does anybody really want to talk about the Middle-East? Or Bosnia? OR the ecological disaster in Latvia and southern Russia?

Scene Three A

(Lights up on JONI *sitting in front of a T V, watching the T V show we've just been listening to. She points the remote and turns the sound off.)*

JONI: Are they letting me off the hook?

*(*ANDY *enters with two drinks—he's been to the refrigerator in the next room, they are somewhere in the White House.)*

ANDY: That's just that show. They put everybody on the hook. and then they let them off, after the commercial. So they can put them back on before the next.

JONI: Where's Ben?

ANDY: He went up to bed.

JONI: Good.
Andy, he knew every move we made. *(Beat)*
How did that come to be?

ACT TWO 57

(ANDY *doesn't answer.*)

JONI: Just tell me.

ANDY: Of course I was talking to him. But it wasn't sinister. He's concerned.

JONI: Let's be calm. All right—let's say I'm J F K—no, let's use someone more recent— (*Clinton comes to mind, is rejected*) —no, not him, not him—let's say I'm George Bush and you're working for me, on something volatile and private. Would you then report it to Barbara?

ANDY: Yes. She scared the hell out of me. All that white hair and weight—formidable.

JONI: Andy, it's possible you have nothing inside you, that you are a completely hollow man. Have you thought about that?

ANDY: No, frankly. All I've thought about is what you're doing and how is it going to turn out and will we get what we want?

JONI: Tell me the absolute truth—completely now. Have you talked to anyone else, including and especially, the Vice President or HIS WIFE?

ANDY: No. We agreed that he must be able to testify that he knew nothing or it will seem like he was in on it to be the incumbent.

JONI: "In on it?" That sounds like you think of it as some sort of scam.

ANDY: Well, it is—I mean, it's a manipulation of sympathy—empathy—to confront and then change the laws.

JONI: And that's a "scam".

ANDY: Well, not necessarily. I mean, "scam" is your term, isn't it?

JONI: I'm sincere.

ANDY: Well, of course. You're sincere about everything you do.

JONI: Am I? In everything? All the time????

ANDY: Well, some things you had to do—to put up with—pretend to be interested in—to get elected, to protect yourself, to— *(Beat)* What do you want with me?

JONI: You tap dance like Bill Robinson—I've never seen anyone tap dance like you.

ANDY: I'm just trying to do my job.

JONI: And what is your job—whom are you serving?

ANDY: You.

JONI: What about her?

ANDY: She's serving you, too.

JONI: Is she?

ANDY: I'm virtually living with her. And she's eager for a date with the President—current and future.

JONI: Eager? She doesn't seem the "eager" type—she seems like the "fuck you" type. And because of you, I made her an actor in our little play, our piece of street theatre that was supposed to change the world. Now, if the press talked to her, directly, all she would say is we had one encounter. And that makes me look like some dupe, some deluded middle-aged woman who thinks a lesbian affair is a kiss and a run through the woods. "Lesbian Love" by Walt Disney. And our possible law-changing Great Moral Event becomes just naive and laughable. And my Parthian shot on my last ride out of the political arena becomes a little pop. Pathetic.

ANDY: Parthian shot?

JONI: Parting shot. Whatever. The Parthians shot and killed thousands on their retreat—

ACT TWO

ANDY: Retreat?

JONI: I *am* leaving this hellish arena.

ANDY: What? I'm doing all this because I want to see you re-elected! How can you even think of leaving? We were—YOU were going to keep the promises that certain past administrations didn't and take possession of this new century. That's the reason I did all this!

JONI: You did all this?

ANDY: Look, all I ever wanted was to be a spokesman—person for you. All I ever wanted was to stand in front of a television camera and speak for the President of the United States—a President like you.

JONI: Okay. Andrew, listen—there are things more important—to me. Not to "The President" —to me! I...have a life, you know? Try to understand—I never loved power for itself enough—I only loved what it can do. And since the mid-term elections, it's been obvious that with this Congress, I won't be able to do anything. You wheel and deal and compromise to make history, but by the time you've gotten somewhere where you can make that history—it's made you. So while I have some shred of an idealistic idea left, I'm using what clout I have to try to start a change. And then I'm going home.

ANDY: With all due respect, Madam President—I mean, I'm hardly a spokesperson for the women of the future, nor would I begin to be—but what about some little girls out there who need your example to—

JONI: "Little girls out there," That's a sweet argument.

ANDY: It's just—I have a daughter, and I've been thinking a lot about her, lately.

JONI: You have a daughter? I didn't know that.

ANDY: *(Lying)* It's...in my file.

JONI: *(Interested, almost excited)* How old? What's her name? Where does she live?

ANDY: She lives with her grandmother. But I don't want to talk about her, what I want to make sure you realize is that in leaving this office—

JONI: I'm hoping they try to fire me.

ANDY: And I'm thinking that if they don't try to impeach you—

JONI: Yes, you can say the word. If they don't try that angle, then I'm still the poster girl for gay rights. And the momentum, at least in the culture, won't be stopped. And that's why we have to keep the momentum going now.

ANDY: Right. And then the people will insist on a next term for you.

JONI: Your optimism is so cute! Like a two-headed calf. Read my lips: no next term. I have other reasons—personal reasons.

(ANDY starts to ask, but JONI let him know it's off limits.)

JONI: So, I'm going back to Vermont, to read a book, take a walk, or something ordinary and wonderful like that. Ride my horses.
You have a child—a daughter.
Ben can't have children. And I'm menopausal now. You're lucky.

ANDY: Yeah.

JONI: Except for the fact you're fired.

ANDY: What?

(JONI realizes what she was waiting to see is on the television—she turns up the volume.)

JONI: Hush. Look—it's Amy Carter. They're interviewing her because of me. I love it. I love it.

ACT TWO 61

I said—you're fired.
I can't trust you. You reported to Ben—about me.

ANDY: But—

JONI: And I found out. Actually, I'm firing you because I found out. You can't control information—isn't it obvious? Ben knew what I was planning. We discussed every thing I was going to do. Do you really think I'd purposely hurt him like that? All he was doing was checking on my sanity, but YOU, you were leaking information, Andrew.
Now you made me miss what Amy was saying.

(ANDY *exits.* JONI *turns down the T V, picks up the phone, presses the button for her bedroom.*)

JONI: *(On phone)* Did I wake you? No? Good. Yeah—Amy Carter. I bet Nightline will top them with Chastity Bono. And now my "misdeeds" have become part of the personal growth of this nation—they're already talking about the "healing." And the issue is dying—killed by coming togetherness and fucking understanding—both of which are fake!! Who do you have to fuck to get some laws changed around here? Don't say it—I broke my own rule. Never have a serious conversation, even with yourself, after eleven P M.
No, he's gone. I fired him.
Of course I had to! We're on our own in this. And, no, he won't turn on me. If he did I'd lose what little faith I have in mankind. There has to be one good person in this world because I'm not it.
I think I'm giving up. I'm coming to bed.

(JONI *hangs up the phone, starts her exit. It rings. She looks puzzled—it's not Ben's extension. She picks it up—*)

JONI: Hello?

(*Lights up on* RACHEL, *talking on a cell phone.*)

RACHEL: You—you gave me this number—remember?

JONI: Oh my god.

RACHEL: I know you used me.

JONI: Rachel—

RACHEL: I want my daughter back. I want a life. Period. I mean, WHAT KIND OF MORALIST ARE YOU?? Sorry, sorry. Don't hang up.

JONI: I'm not a moralist. I'm a politician.

RACHEL: LOOK, I NEED HELP AND I'M NOT GOOD AT ASKING FOR IT!
Sorry, sorry. Don't hang up. I keep yelling. I can't help it.

JONI: I haven't forgotten about you.

RACHEL: *(Running the threats together because she's not comfortable doing it)* I could go to the press I could make a stink I could do horrible things.

JONI: I know.

RACHEL: I could sell my story.

JONI: It's yours to sell. Whenever.

RACHEL: You don't care. About anything?

JONI: I've made my peace with whatever happens. Or doesn't happen, as the case may be.

RACHEL: So I have to be a creep to get something for myself? What am I supposed to do?

JONI: I don't know.

RACHEL: I wish I was back in prison. At least, there I knew the rules! And I had an identity I recognized. I mean, who am I now? Some semi-notorious hooker, like whatshername gave whatshisname movie star the almost blow job except they got busted. I could turn all this into a nice job as a stripper or a security guard.

ACT TWO

What am I qualified to be now? HOW CAN YOU JUST LEAVE PEOPLE HANGING IN THE FUCKING WIND? WHAT KIND OF LIBERAL ARE YOU? ONE WHO ONLY CARES ABOUT PEOPLE IN GENERAL AND NOBODY IN PARTICULAR?? Okay, I've blown it. I'm not sorry. Bye.

(RACHEL *hangs up.* JONI *just sits there with the phone. Then, quickly, she looks at the near future's equivalent of "caller I D" and dials it. Cell phone rings.* RACHEL *is shocked to get the call, but takes it—opens up the cell phone again.*)

RACHEL: Andy?

JONI: Rachel, it's me.

RACHEL: What?

JONI: This is Andy's cell phone number.

RACHEL: I was afraid to call from the apartment.

JONI: Where are you?

RACHEL: I'm afraid to tell you. This is like one of those stories where the F B I comes—

JONI: Oh, for chrissakes, where are you?

RACHEL: Outside—I was on my way to the front door, when I chickened out. Those are big gates. But the house is a lot smaller than I thought.

JONI: Don't move. I'm sending someone out to bring you in.

RACHEL: You sound like a cop.

JONI: I am. I'm the biggest cop in the land. I'm the mother of all cops. Now don't move!!

RACHEL: *(Daunted)* 'Kay.

(RACHEL *turns off the cell phone and waits.* JONI *pushes another button on her phone.*)

JONI: Chester? There's a young woman—
Right. That's her.
Bring her to your office.
Thanks.

(RACHEL *"sees" one of Chester's minions motioning for her to come to them. She exits towards them.* JONI *pushes another button on her phone, to talk to Ben.*)

JONI: Ben?
Oh, that's okay, sweetheart. Go back to sleep. I'll see you in the morning.

(JONI *hangs up her phone and exits. End of scene*)

Scene Three B

(RACHEL *is sitting and smoking, just as she was in the first scene of the play, but she's holding a huge, elegant ashtray, maybe antique. She hears* JONI *in the next room.*)

JONI: *(To Chester, offstage)* Thanks, Chester.

(JONI *enters.* RACHEL *stands immediately and accidently dumps the ashtray.*)

RACHEL: Fuck.

JONI: It's all right. Don't clean it up. They'll get it.

RACHEL: Okay.

JONI: They have big vacuums.

RACHEL: "They."

JONI: Oh, please spare me the attitude about who cleans the damn place!!
You're right.

RACHEL: About what?

JONI: About what kind of liberal I am. But I want you to know I do care about someone in particular. I'm not as heartless as you make me sound.

ACT TWO

RACHEL: Look, Joni, Madam President, whatever. You can afford a therapist. You can afford your own private fucking priest or whatever it is you use. I mean, is everything you do just for show? I mean, you had me believing all this crap. What was that? Justice Interruptus? You sacrificed my life for this humanitarian issue you supposedly care so much about!

(Beat)

JONI: I have a proposition. Would you like to be the President's girlfriend—for real?

RACHEL: Couldn't you just get me a computer job somewhere?

JONI: I want to go all the way—publicly—with this. I want to make it real. Undeniable. Unavoidable. I want to make a stand.

RACHEL: But then I'd be publicly gay, forever.

JONI: That's right. And so would I.

RACHEL: How can this help me get my daughter back?

JONI: Trust me.

RACHEL: You must think I'm an idiot.

JONI: No.

RACHEL: How can I trust you??
You and your world are scarier than prison.

JONI: What other choice do you have?

RACHEL: Okay—I'm more comfortable now—it sounds like prison negotiations, but just without the weapons and the profanity.

JONI: Look, Bitch, it's fucking hard for fucking me to fucking trust anyone, either. Okay? That better?

RACHEL: …Yeah.

JONI: I'll send a car for you at noon. Tomorrow. Okay?

(Beat)

RACHEL: What are we going to…do?

JONI: I have two public appearances and you'll be with me.

RACHEL: *(Sincere)* Jesus. What shall I wear? I don't have anything—wait—I've got those outfits Andy and I bought. YOU BETTER NOT BE DICKING WITH ME!!

JONI: I'm not "dicking" with you.

RACHEL: Okay. Tomorrow. I trust you. We go public and I'll be able to get my daughter back. I trust you. Right now I have no other options. I trust you. I have no power but tomorrow that will change. I trust you. It's like a mantra—it sounds like a mantra…

JONI: That's because it's an act of faith. I told the truth when I told the press I think I love you, Rachel. I do—you're very dear.

RACHEL: You don't have to love me.

JONI: I know. Chester will get you home.

RACHEL: Okay.

JONI: Good night. Friends?

RACHEL: I don't know—you got some mouth on you, girl. Okay. 'Night.

(JONI *exits to go to bed.* RACHEL *can't stand it—she bends down and cleans up the ashes.*)

(End of scene)

Scene Four

(ANDY *enters a room, carrying a Tower Records bag.*)

ACT TWO 67

ANDY: Rachel? Rachel? *(He looks for her—doesn't find her, isn't happy about it.)* Dammit! Dammit!!

(ANDY takes off his suitcoat and tie, fixes himself a drink, then begins to unwrap the C Ds and tapes. He stacks them up neatly and then pops a cassette tape into the player. He leans back as if to listen to music and relax and uses the remote to start the player, then realizes the tape needs rewinding—rewinds with the remote—and clicks "play." What he hears is not music but most of the previous conversation between RACHEL and JONI.)

(JONI and RACHEL on tape from ANDY's sound system)

RACHEL: I could go to the press I could make a stink I could do horrible things.

JONI: I know.

RACHEL: I could sell my story.

JONI: It's yours to sell. Whenever.

RACHEL: You don't care. About anything?

JONI: I've made my peace with whatever happens.

RACHEL: So I have to be a creep to get something for myself? What am I supposed to do?

(ANDY stops the tape and rewinds it, hits "play" again.)

RACHEL: LOOK, I NEED HELP AND I'M NOT GOOD AT ASKING FOR IT! Sorry, sorry, don't hang up. I keep yelling. I can't help it.

JONI: I haven't forgotten about you.

(ANDY can't stand what he's hearing. Fast forwards it, hits "play" again.)

JONI: Where are you?

RACHEL: I'm afraid to tell you. This is like one of those stories where the F B I comes—

JONI: Oh, for Chrissakes, where are you?

RACHEL: Outside—I was on my way to the front door, when I chickened out. Those are big gates. But the house is a lot smaller than I thought.

ANDY: *(To the absent* RACHEL*)* Don't play this game. You can't play this game.

(ANDY *sits for a beat or two. The door opens and* RACHEL *enters with cigarettes and a bottle of Stoli.)*

RACHEL: *(Indicating the vodka and cigarettes)* Dinner.

ANDY: How did you get through the reporters?

RACHEL: I gave them a photo op. And they let me go.

ANDY: You let them take your picture?

RACHEL: Many, many pictures.

ANDY: But that will look so forward! You could have, at least, tried to run from them.

RACHEL: "Forward!" What are you, some school mistress? Some male nun? As if—I'm going to run demurely and upset across the street, my tits bouncing with every step? "Ooooo bad papparazzi, go away! I want my privacy!"

ANDY: Whatever.

RACHEL: Oh my god, are you actually off duty for a while? *(Puts bottle and cigarettes down, smiles at* ANDY. *She notices the "Tower Records" bag.)* Still indulging your addiction, I see?

ANDY: *(Covering what he's been doing)* Re-mastered Ella. *(He flicks on the C D player with the remote—music comes up.)*

ANDY: I hope you don't trust her too much.

RACHEL: Who?

ANDY: Who.

ACT TWO   69

RACHEL: I'm supposed to trust her and you.
Everybody's trustworthy. "In God we Trust." And we
all know how trustworthy he's been.

ANDY: She fired me.

RACHEL: What?
How can she do that?
(Answers her own question)
Oh well, yeah—
She can't touch your health plan and stuff, can she?

ANDY: Yeah. She can.

RACHEL: What's going on?

ANDY: I don't know.

RACHEL: But you always know everything.

ANDY: Are you meeting with her? On the sly?

RACHEL: "On the sly?" "On the sly?" In the midst of all
this deception, you're accusing me of doing something
"on the sly?" I've forgotten which side I'm on! I
thought I was luring the President into an adulterous,
lesbian affair to check on her sexuality, so "we" or
"they" —the ever-present "they" would know if she
was putting the national security at risk, but then—
wo—she one-ups us, at least I THINK it was a one-up
and not planned all along, but SHE comes out as a gay
woman and outs me, too. And then you lure me back
into this town to live with you to prove to my mother
and her lawyer, so you say, that I'm het-er-o-sex-ual
and trust-worthy, so I can get my daughter back into
my life—this new life I'm supposed to have because
you're fixing it up for me. And then you announce that
you, my ticket to this new life, have been fired. I think
that's my cue to grab the nearest source of buoyancy
and hold on for dear life!

ANDY: You're meeting with her tomorrow.

RACHEL: It's not a meeting—it's a date. How did you know that? *(She doesn't even pursue it.)* Do you also know that she said she loves me?

ANDY: You're an idiot.

RACHEL: Some people say "I love you" and mean it.

ANDY: You've bought the hype. She's always in a press conference, even when she's alone! "Her name is Rachel. And I love her. We haven't had sex yet—"

RACHEL: We'll see about that, won't we?
I deserve a cigarette.
Oh, here's your cell phone.

(RACHEL *lights up.* ANDY *takes his cell phone and exits, slamming the door.)*

RACHEL: Right.

(End of scene)

Scene Five

(ANDY *is on his cell phone somewhere anonymous and uncomfortable.)*

ANDY: Ben?
I thought this was his private number…
I'm sorry.
Yeah—he has my cell phone number, if—
Tell him I hope he feels better.
(He disconnects, frustrated, dials another number.)
Mom!
No, I'm fine.
I'm stressed because I'm busy.
No, I just called…how you're doing?
You do? Oh—well, you'd better get back to work then.
No, I'm fine. Everything is fine.
If you call my number—I'm in the office now—if you call my number, a woman might answer the phone.

ACT TWO

Don't I wish—. She's just staying there.—
What'd you think about our press conference? I was there by the—
Yeah, she's incredible.
Yeah, she nailed him all right, and with something I—
Yeah, she's pretty amazing, but it was my—
Yeah.
A shoe-in. Can't wait for the campaign. And I'll—
Oh, of course—I forgot—sorry—hope you make your deadline.
Oh, I know you never miss one.
Mom?
(But she has hung up. He loses all heart—hits bottom. Then pulls himself together to make one more call.)
ANDY: Just give me his voice mail.
Ben? I'm just leaving this message for you. It's Andy. I'm out of the loop, man. She cut me.
I'm out of the loop.
(He folds up his cell phone and just stands there—nowhere to go)
(End of scene)

Scene Six

*(Sound of a sexual climax. Lights up several beats later, after they've recovered completely—*JONI *and* RACHEL *in bed in a bedroom in the White House. They have just made love. A long silence)*

RACHEL: That was nice—I've been—really lonely.

JONI: Me, too.

(Long silence)

RACHEL: I guess I thought we were just going to go to a function, I didn't—

JONI: You seduced me, I believe.

RACHEL: I believe it was mutual. Well, Miss Pinot Grigio helped.

(Beat)

JONI: Well, now no one can deny that you're the President's girlfriend. We're almost going steady. But now I've muddied the waters with adultery. Clarity and passion—they don't go together. They fight, in fact. *(Beat)* Rachel?

RACHEL: It's just I don't feel comfortable talking about anything here.

JONI: The bedrooms aren't bugged.

RACHEL: Every place is bugged. Didn't they get Nixon with some tapes?

JONI: They never got Nixon. He escaped to a foreign country.

RACHEL: I thought he just went home to southern California.

JONI: Yes.

RACHEL: But didn't they get him on tape somewhere in the White House?

JONI: Not the bedroom. The Nixons never used the bedroom.

RACHEL: Where did they sleep?

JONI: He slept in a coffin filled with dirt from a landfill in Yorba Linda. And she—well, I was always hoping she was bunking with the housekeeper or one of those really young pages.

RACHEL: Which gender?

JONI: Female, of course. Why do you ask?

RACHEL: Female, of course.

ACT TWO 73

JONI: It's so nice having you here. It's been a long time for me.

RACHEL: How long?

JONI: I was twenty.

RACHEL: That's a long time. But, in between, you had—

JONI: Ben. And others along the road—I'm very, very old, you know.

RACHEL: Other women?

JONI: 'Course. *(Quick change of subject)* I've been thinking about your case.

RACHEL: Case is over. I was sentenced and I served, would probably still be serving if it weren't for you. *(Remembers* ANDY*)* Or...somebody.

JONI: You should have gotten a sentencing attorney. They cost about eight thousand dollars, but it's the only way to keep from getting a really punitive sentence.

RACHEL: It's supposed to be "punitive" —it's prison. Or, as I called it, "home".

(Beat)

JONI: "Home." How many places have you been able to call home? Before that?

RACHEL: Jesus! What do you think I am? Rough trade?

JONI: What?

RACHEL: Is that what you think I am?

JONI: I don't know what that is.

RACHEL: I'm not some street urchin! I supported myself for years.

JONI: But you were alone.

RACHEL: I've always been alone. Until Jennifer was born.

JONI: And you met your roommate Sheri?

RACHEL: So—so—you're trying to win some humanitarian award?

JONI: I'm trying to be human, yes. When will Sheri get out and what will she do?

RACHEL: No.
She'll be in C C C in a year or so. That's not long. Of course they'll drug test her every week, so she'll have to clean up or go back in. Your Congress cut everything, you know—

JONI: "My Congress."

RACHEL: Well, there's nothing to fucking do in there except take drugs! They cut the athletics and the classes and anything that might resemble rehabilitation. The only thing left to do is to get addicted and then go to de-tox. Some rich, white prick goes to prison for ripping off old ladies, the news shows him in some minimum-security facility and everyone thinks all prisons are country clubs! And then one of your fucking colleagues gets up and pontificates about "getting tough on crime" and gets re-elected by taking more away from the prison population which are sixty percent brown people with no skills when they fucking get out!

(JONI *gets up, with a sheet wrapped around her, and leaves the room.*)

RACHEL: Joni—Joni—I don't blame you. Completely. But I can't pretend that I'm not angry.

(JONI *returns, still in the sheet, looking at a folder.*)

RACHEL: What's that?

JONI: Your file print-out. *(Reading it)* So your roommate—Sheri Montoya—was not in for cellular or computer access fraud.

ACT TWO

RACHEL: No, they wouldn't put two cyber criminals together.

JONI: *(Reading the sentencing)* It's just a felony—how did she end up in a federal facility?

RACHEL: Her lawyer got the Feds to pick up her charges.

JONI: It was a trade off?

(Somewhere in here RACHEL gets out of bed, too—and also wrapped in a sheet.)

RACHEL: Yeah—less time in a state facility or more time but in a more humane and low-security environment. What are you doing?

JONI: I'm thinking of an appeal for sentence reduction. She hasn't been in that long—it's right at the deadline.

RACHEL: Can you do that? Get a sentence reduction after somebody's inside?

JONI: A good lawyer can—one who's not President. *(She pushes the button on her telephone, talks to someone.)*
Yeah. Cooper?
I have a case for that young firm you know.
Pro-bono—personal favor.
Looks pretty straightforward.
You can start on the brief tomorrow?
Thanks.
(She hangs up the phone.)

RACHEL: So that's power.

JONI: That's why people want it.

RACHEL: Thank you.

JONI: Thank you.

RACHEL: Why are you thanking me?

JONI: Let's just say I feel less like a plastic garbage bag and more like a bird—a barely alive bird, but a bird,

nevertheless.
So your "roommate" hasn't been in that long. That's good for sentence reduction, but you haven't known her...

RACHEL: It only takes a couple of days to know you—you know—like someone.

JONI: Or love her.

RACHEL: *(About the file)* What does that file say about me?

JONI: *(Handing it to her)* Here.

RACHEL: *(Studying different items in her file)* Wow. My credit rating sucks.
Look! They kept track of individual payments on that stupid motorcycle.
Wo. Grades—everything.
Jesus! I'd completely forgotten about this episode—now, that's wrong here.
Here's the crime file...
Ah—"relevant conduct"—that's what put me away. I only hacked into one system in three tries, but because they found stuff that could be used for code abuse and general computer trespass, they assumed "relevant conduct"—that I was doing it all the time because I could. And they don't have to prove that part. And then asshole Harry went ahead and kept working on the full hacking job which became the "joint venture" that added to my sentence and put him away for two years. And then they hit us both with a special skill enhancement and added six more months—all because we had both once worked in lawful, gainful employment in the computer field. They punish you, big time, for having the secret knowledge of the sacred pathway and then using it for ill.

JONI: And they should—punish you.

ACT TWO

RACHEL: What? But it's not fair!

JONI: What's not fair is having special knowledge or power and then not using it.

RACHEL: Are you lecturing me?

JONI: No, I'm lecturing myself.

RACHEL: Joni—

JONI: Uh-huh.

RACHEL: You're not gay—you're not a gay woman, are you?

(Long pause)

JONI: No, I'm not. But people need to think I am.

RACHEL: *(Beat)* Yes.

JONI: How could you tell? Wasn't I—

RACHEL: No hunger. Just "special knowledge." No real passion. For me.

JONI: But real affection and…intensity…? Didn't I do it right?

RACHEL: *(Amused)* "It."

JONI: I've been very lonely, Rachel. Physically lonely all the time. It's so nice—you. Skin on skin. Warm breath. Amorphous sexual identity like when I was at school. And young.

RACHEL: But I thought you were so doing it, like with Andy—you know, I thought you said so in the bathroom at the restaurant.

JONI: Oh, I was just pretending to have a sex life—to be more than just a head on top of a body encased in very nice—

RACHEL: —expensive—

JONI: —clothes. When Ben and I envisioned this, the plan was just to be publicly gay—I never thought I'd actually—

RACHEL: —have to have sex?

JONI: Get to. I feel so…good.

RACHEL: Great. Now how do we get my daughter back? That's my trade off.

JONI: You're tough.

RACHEL: I'm desperate.

JONI: We need to create a big event where we can be seen, unequivocally, as a couple. Not being together at some function or "caught having dinner" or "caught sneaking into a limo." Something with moral authority. Something courageous. Something pure, so they can't deny us, so they have to take us just as we are. And then, book you onto every talk show in the free world.

RACHEL: And this means?

JONI: Real power.
In the meantime, don't go—I don't want to let go of you—just yet.

(They hold the embrace.)

(End of scene)

Scene Seven

(In a darkish area with eerie, almost neon light. ANDY is in civvies and holding a major silver-looking .33 Magnum hand gun. He takes a deep breath, gets ready. Sound of a limo driving up, stopping, then a strange wind sound, and he aims the pistol quickly and efficiently and starts to shoot. For a terrible moment, we might think he's gone "DanWhite" and is shooting at a real human target. The gun makes a not-too-loud popping sound with every shot,

ACT TWO

accompanied by human screams. RACHEL *enters from behind, watches him, shakes her head in disapproval.)*

RACHEL: You gotta kill all the alien zombies in the big house first or they'll get you. Then the cloned humans. Then shoot out all the limo tires and you'll get a weapon upgrade. Okay, you're dead. It's an evil game. Doesn't give you an inch.

ANDY: *(Turns around and faces her—he's like a little boy who's stunned, he's so overwhelmed with the events of his life)* You have to marry me.

*(*RACHEL *stands completely still for several beats.)*

RACHEL: You're pregnant.

ANDY: It's not funny.

RACHEL: Tell me about it.

ANDY: You shut me out. Admit it, just once, Rachel. You could have called me. You could have told me.

RACHEL: No.

ANDY: Why not?

RACHEL: I'm gay.

ANDY: You're gay.

RACHEL: I'm gay.

ANDY: But I want my daughter. I want my family.

RACHEL: We never were a family, Andy. Never. We were never a family. Never, never, never. We were barely a couple. We exchanged some bodily fluids and then went back to our obsessions. A lot of people do that. Some of them get married. To each other. We went back to work. It's no big deal.

ANDY: Then what is a big deal? Rachel? Something needs to be a big deal. Everything's fake, Rachel.

RACHEL: Not eveything, Andy. Some things are... lethal.

ANDY: You're gay.

RACHEL: Right.

ANDY: She's not.

RACHEL: I know.

ANDY: Anybody in love?

RACHEL: I am—with Sheri.

ANDY: Roommate.

RACHEL: You surprised?

ANDY: No. I knew you weren't in love with me. I knew there was something...
I had this idea—a hundred years ago—that I would save you. You would come out, with Joan, and we'd, maybe even, change the way people are treated and...

RACHEL: —your mother'd be proud.

ANDY: And now all I want is my daughter. Under that stupid pink barrette is this entire world and I'm missing it. I've already missed seven—six years of it.

RACHEL: Well, it is seven, if you count the pregnancy, which you also missed.

ANDY: That's not my fault! That's your fault!

RACHEL: All right. Yes.

ANDY: At last. *(Beat)* Doesn't help anything. Does it?

RACHEL: No.

ANDY: I can't even get angry, anymore—it's just stupid and sad.

RACHEL: Andy?

ANDY: Huh?

RACHEL: Everything's gonna be all right.

ACT TWO   81

ANDY: You don't know that.

RACHEL: Sure I do.

ANDY: How?

RACHEL: My appointment's been approved—whether she's really gay or not, I'm the President's girlfriend and everyone in the world, from Sri Lanka to Akron, Ohio, will know it. Talk shows, action figures, I am Ambassadoress of Gaydonia. So, put down the gun and let's get out of here. I have to have a cigarette soon or I will kill someone with something.

ANDY: Okay.

RACHEL: Give back the gun. It's major. You must've left your driver's license to get it.

ANDY: Okay.

RACHEL: Give it to that kid with the pimples—I think he works here.

ANDY: Okay.

RACHEL: Come on...

(ANDY *and* RACHEL *exit—he follows her like a docile child.*)

(End of scene)

Scene Eight

(JONI *is in the garden again.* ANDY *enters, still in his civvies.*)

JONI: This was my husband's idea.

(ANDY *doesn't say anything.*)

JONI: He says I use people.

(No comment from ANDY*)*

JONI: You're not fired.

ANDY: Thanks.

JONI: I know you started reporting to Ben because he convinced you I might be nuts. That I was under too much pressure and flailing around to try to regain some sense of—what—ownership of this office. And he was right, except for the "nuts" part. I've been more than nuts—I've been completely crazy. Ben is dying and we've known it for several months. I'll finish my term, of course, and then we're going to go home and spend some time together. It may be too late now, but I'd like to step beyond all these false starts and use all my special knowledge of the machinery of this town to do something completely idealistic, history-making—and go out with a bang instead of whimper. As a private citizen, everything about me will be just eccentric or quaint— "geezer news" —my life will have little impact. I'll be an oddity, a "highly-regarded toastmistress" —some completely toothless icon of something that people can agree with all they want, in safety, because there will be no legislation to back up anyone's claim for a gay lifestyle. Because, Andy, because in a democracy, opinions only carry weight if they pass legislation or set a legal precedent. You can't protect anyone with opinions.

ANDY: So, what do we do?

JONI: Is it possible? To heat it up again?

ANDY: The news from Southern Russia is pretty terrible. I think questions about your sexuality would be an easy sell. So, we're trying to basically, piss off Congress so they'll come and get you.

JONI: That's it.

ANDY: It's harder than I thought.

JONI: It's the Senate. They're tired—from the last time.

ANDY: Couldn't we just tell the public the truth?

ACT TWO

JONI: What a nutty, nutty idea.

ANDY: It is something we haven't tried.

JONI: Tell everyone I lied to them again about my sexuality and come out as a straight person? No, I'm a gay woman for the rest of my life. That's my story and I'm sticking to it.

ANDY: So how do we heat it up again?

JONI: I've been flaunting my relationship with Rachel publicly, just everywhere—but all of that is just tabloid fodder. It's all just snickered at. What do I have to do? Kiss Rachel on Jerry Falwell's front lawn?

ANDY: Too many lawn ornaments. Joke.

JONI: Funny.

ANDY: But something on their turf would do it. I mean, that's the nest to stick the stick into.

JONI: But it would have to be respectable—whatever it is; whatever we do.

ANDY: But very confrontational.

JONI: Right. Some action or appearance that confronts them at the very center of their belief.

ANDY: That they can't deny.

JONI: Shit! I've got to finish that speech on the water emergency in inland Estonia. Can you believe they have to haul water from the ocean and boil out the impurities so they can baptize babies without poisoning them? Meanwhile, we waste water on this fucking garden which I hate! The red flowers go there and the yellow ones go there and the bushes go right there and it's all so anal—as if we could control nature! As if we could control life!

ANDY: I'm so sorry about Ben.

JONI: You didn't know?

ANDY: No.

JONI: He didn't tell you?

ANDY: No.

JONI: You see? You see? That's why losing him is going to be so very bad. He's the only person I've ever known who could really keep a secret.

(JONI *sits in silent grief.* ANDY *reaches out awkwardly, hesistantly, and pats her on the shoulder.*)

JONI: What?

ANDY: Nothing.

JONI: Thanks. *(Suddenly, in complete frustration)* What does it take to piss off the religious right? Appear naked in church!!!?

ANDY: Naked before God.

JONI: What?

ANDY: Naked before God might do it.

JONI: What are you thinking?

ANDY: Baptism. They have to take you.

JONI: But I'm a Quaker.

ANDY: If the two of you presented yourselves together, as a couple—

JONI: Quakers don't believe in baptism.

ANDY: —and walked up to the altar, they have to take you in.

JONI: But my family's been Quaker for seven generations.

ANDY: Even if they separate you, the action of walking up there together—that image is so potent, indelible.

JONI: That would be like giving up my soul.

ANDY: To regain it.

JONI: You're manipulating me—

ANDY: John Lennon and Yoko Ono.

JONI: Et tu, Andrew. *(Really looks at him)* What have I created in you?

(He smiles with satisfaction.)

(End of scene)

Scene Nine

(Sound of a Baptist service going on—singing and clapping. The preacher then starts to speak—we only hear his voice. An offstage "light" shows us where the altar is.)

PREACHER'S VOICE: Lord God. We come before you today to ask you—yes—to ask you to move the hearts of anyone here who is lonely and afraid and in sin but too shy to come forth, too frightened that your love will not be there for them, too afraid to come up and stand before Your altar and be baptized and receive Your perfect love. Dear Father, we ask You to move those lonely souls to come up here, to your altar, and accept, your son, Jesus Christ as their personal saviour, and be baptized in His Holy Name. Amen. Now to help them along, let's sing, people—let's sing "Just As I Am"—because that is all we are before God. Ourselves.

PREACHER'S VOICE & CONGREGATION: *(Singing)* Just as I am, Oh Lord to thee…

(From the back of the "church", through the audience, come JONI and RACHEL, holding hands, walking up to the altar. The singing of the hymn peters out as the "congregation" sees who is coming up to be saved. As JONI and RACHEL disappear into the "light" offstage, the singing stops completely and all we hear is silence, then "congregational unrest".)

(End of scene)

Scene Ten

("Congregational Unrest" grows into a crowd shouting. ANDY walks out to lots of camera flashes, opens a piece of paper and reads it.)

ANDY: The President is resting calmly. She is not under any form of sedation. What has been called a nervous breakdown is neither from nerves nor a breakdown. The President wants to make it clear that her actions at the Living Word of God Baptist Church and the actions of the young woman with whom she's been involved were sincere and not meant to be sacrilegious in any way. Coming forth and asking for baptism, with the young woman with whom she has been involved, was the President's way of showing her unshakable belief in the purity and rightness of her Lesbian relationship before the only true judge of moral rightness—God. She also commends the quick response of the choirmaster, Mr Lance Boudine, who used his body as a shield allowing the aforementioned young woman to escape injury from the flying hymnals. The outpouring of support and concern from some members of the congregation of the Living Word of God Baptist Church has been very heartening and offsets the somewhat vitriolic attacks which were the only ones covered by the national news media. Now the President would like to rest. It is, after all, Sunday. Thank you.

(More flashes and shouting of questions, but ANDY folds up the paper, puts it in his jacket, and exits)

(End of scene)

Scene Eleven

ACT TWO

(RACHEL *is sitting on the couch, reading from several books.* ANDY *enters from another room, carrying a Curious George book*)

RACHEL: Do you consider sexual intercourse a form of colonization on the part of the male?

ANDY: I—I prefer not to think of it that way.

RACHEL: Well, of course you don't—I mean, who would? But this woman has got a point.

ANDY: Are you sure you need to read all this? Where did you get these?

RACHEL: They're all references from the back of your mother's fucking book.

ANDY: Oh.

RACHEL: I mean, these women are very smart, that I've been reading here, and I want to know what they say just in case—

ANDY: Regis and Cathy Lee are not going to ask you about any of this, believe me. They just want to talk about your interview on Barbara Walters.

RACHEL: I was an idiot an Barbara Walters! But she was like this guidance counselor I had—Mrs Bauer— who was always getting me into her office and then leaning on me to confess, confess, confess to smoking in the girls' room which, of course, I was. So I'd spill my guts which of course I did. But not on national television!

ANDY: I think it was good for America. And most of the kids were in bed.

RACHEL: But not for "Good Morning, America"— Luckily, I only had fifteen seconds to sum up my life and everything I thought about everything, sitting in this cubicle, smaller than anything in prison, baking under these lights, sound check, "Speak!" How do you stand it?

ANDY: It doesn't happen to me, Rachel. I'm the guy behind the guy behind the scenes. And I like it that way.

RACHEL: Is she going to run again?

ANDY: Since Ben is gone, she just wants peace and quiet. And besides the people will never forgive her for cheating on him.

RACHEL: That's so the double standard! What if I'd been a man? Or she was?

ANDY: That is so— *(Decides to illustrate just how stupid her comment is with available objects)* —all right, all right. Okay. *(Gathering the objects)* This is you. This is her. This is Ben. *(Separating the objects into categories)* The gay people go here. And the straight people go there. These are the men—man. These are the women. So this one—her—we change to male and he sleeps with this one—you who's still female. So this female we changed to a male isn't gay anymore.

RACHEL: But, in this case, never really was, I think. But went about it in such a methodical and expert way— like someone with really excellent fine motor skills playing a piano furiously, but with no discernible… tune.

ANDY: You mean like Schoenberg?

RACHEL: No, I mean, like a vibrator.

ANDY: Back to our…diagram. So that one is still President.

RACHEL: And married to that one, when he was still alive.

ANDY: And then we change you to a man… And then what do we have?

RACHEL: A coffee cup.

ANDY: A television remote.

ACT TWO

RACHEL: A cordless telephone.

(The phone rings in RACHEL's *hand—she answers it.)*

RACHEL: Hello?
Oh, hi hon.
Good. Great.
Bye.
(To ANDY, *really happy)*
Sheri's coming over.

ANDY: *(Not thrilled)* Oh good. *(Doesn't really want to leave)* And don't worry about the television appearances. You're great on them. You're yourself. Charlie Rose will only want to talk about your book.

RACHEL: "Book." As if I'd actually sat down and wrote it. And he'll have read it, too. Jesus. And he's smart.

ANDY: No, that's good. Because he tends to ask these really long convoluted questions and it will give you time to think. Just listen for the verb.

RACHEL: Will you be watching?

ANDY: I'll be in Riga—I'm covering the whole conference. I'd better get home—it's an early flight.

RACHEL: Jennifer fall asleep no problem?

ANDY: No problem.

RACHEL: Should I—

ANDY: No. She's sound asleep.

RACHEL: *(About what's on television)* It's the end of the Gay Pride March.

ANDY: We'll go next year when you're not so recognizable.

RACHEL: I'll be able to go with Sheri by then.

ANDY: Right.

RACHEL: Why did Joni cancel on them?

ANDY: She wants to send a clear message—she's retiring from politics.

RACHEL: *(Getting him to sit down)* Oh stop hovering.

ANDY: Why are we looking at people wandering around some folding chairs?

RACHEL: And whose butt is that in front of the camera?

ANDY: It's C-Span. Get a real channel. *(He clicks it.)*

VOICE OF A GAY FEMALE CELEB: If a mediocre actor like Ronald Reagan could be President, why couldn't a really good comedian like Ellen Degeneres win and for next term?

RACHEL: Wait—there's Joni!

JONI: *(Voice)* She's smarter and god knows, funnier than Reagan. I'd endorse her! As a gay woman, I'd like to say she's much better-looking than any President we've had so far!

VOICE OF A GAY FEMALE CELEB: Except Hillary, of course! AND you Joan!

(Cheers from the crowd)

ANDY: What is she doing?

JONI: *(Voice)* You're too kind. And I'd have those glasses checked. But thank you.

(Laughter from the audience)

JONI: *(Voice)* People have been in measuring the windows in the Oval for new curtains, but I've epoxied the poster of Jodi Foster to the wall so my successor will have a tough time getting it down.

(Laughter and applause)

ANDY: What is she doing?

JONI: *(Voice)* It's been a strange couple of years. Um—I want to tell you how much all the expressions of

ACT TWO

love and sympathy that I received when Ben passed away—how very much they meant to me. He was a remarkable man, my best friend and companion. But he, of all people, wouldn't want me to give up and go home. I wasn't going to come today but I just had to. I had to be here to watch the world change.

(*Cheers and applause.* ANDY *turns off the television.*)

RACHEL: Does that mean she's back in the running?

ANDY: I don't know. She said I'd be the first to know—meaning, I thought—there's no chance in hell. Do you hear a phone ringing for me? Oh well, I'll know soon enough.

RACHEL: She's a closeted heterosexual. She's the only closeted heterosexual I know of! And they love her!

ANDY: I guess she's gay for life now.

RACHEL: It feels like a circus.

ANDY: It is a circus.

RACHEL: And now I'm part of it..

ANDY: We all are, whether we want to be or not..

RACHEL: Jesus! I wish I'd read some of these books before I told anyone anything.

ANDY: The truth of your life is more powerful than anything in these books.

RACHEL: No, it's not. It's just another soap opera. Without some context, it's just a story. Your mother's right about the purpose of theory in social change.

ANDY: Just stop. Right there. I can't take it from both sides, Rachel! I'm sorry about history—I really am! I'm sorry about my penis! I'm sorry about weapons! I'm sorry about the havoc testosterone has wrought! But men aren't completely hopeless, you know. A lot of good civilized things have come from our stupid hands and dumb brains. Look—Curious George is a male and so is the man with the yellow hat. And that little girl in there loves them! And she loves me too, I think!

RACHEL: Of course she does, Andy.

ANDY: And goddamit, I saved your life!

RACHEL: Well—

ANDY: Just admit it, please!

RACHEL: Yes.

ANDY: And I'm sorry about the sperm seven years ago, but NO, I'm not sorry about that because that was the best thing that has ever happened to me!!!

RACHEL: Me too.

ANDY: Really?

RACHEL: Of course. How can you even ask such a stupid question?

ANDY: How is it I always lose the argument even when we agree? How does this happen?

RACHEL: You're so irritating. Because you won't go away. And now you won't ever!

(Impasse—the truth)

ANDY: I don't think you're supposed to wear the nicotine patch at the same time you're chewing the nicotine gum.

RACHEL: I'm—doing—the—best—I—can. If I'm ever going to have a computer job, I've got to quit smoking.

ANDY: You're doing well.

RACHEL: Don't—patronize—me.

ANDY: Oh why not?

RACHEL: I—am—sorry.

ACT TWO

ANDY: No you're not. *(Beat)* It wouldn't kill you to be happy for once, Rachel. You know?

RACHEL: You first.

ANDY: *(About the Curious George book)* A man and a woman worked on this together and it has a happy ending!

RACHEL: It's a kid's book!

ANDY: Will you ever let anyone have the last word?

RACHEL: When I hear something I can't argue with!

(ANDY kisses her on the forehead and gets to the door, hoping to have the last word.)

ANDY: Good bye.

RACHEL: *(She beats him at the who-has-the-last-word game.)* 'Night!

(He leaves. She picks up the clicker and turns the TV back on. It's JONI—RACHEL considers calling ANDY, decides not to. She listens.)

JONI: *(On stage, in front of a mike)* When I was a young student I went to what was then the Soviet Union and there I was asked by another young student, a Russian, what it was like living in a democracy. I guess I was tired of being a spokesperson for America, so I just said, "It's noisy." I think it's important to remember that as we go into a new campaign season. Silence is bad, except for meditation and I guess, sleep. Some people have been talking a lot about the war for control of the culture—I think it was me, actually. Anyway, long live partisanship, as long as I get to keep mine. I'm not interested in consensus or finding a common ground with some of the factions in this country. I have nothing in common with the Aryan Nation or Focus on the Family, but history and geography have stuck us together. In fact, we're all stuck with each other, and as more and more family members—yes, I did say family—as more of the family arrives from all over the world, diversity may be the only consistency. So please just look for a President of the United States, not a President of the United Culture. We will never have a United Culture. We will never be a "people." We will always argue, and, sometimes viciously. You're waiting for me to say, "But…" and end on a positive note. But I already have. The good news is the *noise*.

(Lots of cheering and applause, but RACHEL *cuts it off. She picks up the Curious George book and starts to look at it—the pleasure of it taking her over, in spite of herself.)*

END OF PLAY